"I HAVE A DREAM"

"I Have a Dream"

The quotations of
MARTIN LUTHER KING JR.

Compiled and edited by LOTTE HOSKINS

Publishers   GROSSET & DUNLAP   *New York*

"I HAVE A DREAM"

·· A ··

ACQUIESCENCE

The Negro cannot win the respect of his oppressor by acquiescing; he merely increases the oppressor's arrogance and contempt. Acquiescence is interpreted as proof of the Negro's inferiority. The Negro cannot win the respect of the white people of the South or the peoples of the world if he is willing to sell the future of his children for his personal and immediate comfort and safety.

ACTION

Any real change in the status quo depends on continued creative action to sharpen the conscience of the nation and establish a climate in which even the most recalcitrant elements are forced to admit that change is necessary.

. . . **Direct and Legal.** Direct action is not a substitute for work in the courts and the halls of government. Bringing about passage of a new and broad law by a city council, state legislature or the Congress, or pleading cases before the courts of the land, does not eliminate the necessity for bringing about the mass dramatization of injustice in front of a city hall. Indeed, direct action and legal action complement one another; when skillfully employed, each becomes more effective.

. . . **Self-Help.** When Moses strove to lead the Israelites to the Promised Land, God made it clear that he would not do for them what they could do for themselves.

ADVERTISING

Advertisers have long since learned that most people are softminded, and they capitalize on this susceptibility with skillful and effective slogans.

ALTRUISM

Every man must decide whether he will walk in the light of creative altruism or the darkness of destructive selfishness. This is the judgment. Life's most persistent and urgent question is, "What are you doing for others?"‹

AMERICA

It is the strength of America, and more importantly its people utilizing that indispensable ingredient of relentless and insistent struggle characteristic of American democracy, which causes evil to be exposed and ultimately overcome. It is these struggles, in the composite, which constitute the finest hours of American history.

. . . **Brotherhood.** I have a dream . . . It is a dream deeply rooted in the American dream . . . I have a dream that one day in the red hills of Georgia, sons of former slaves and the sons of former slave owners will be able to sit down together at the table of brotherhood.

. . . **Civil Rights.** The mere fact that we live in the United States means that we are caught in a network of inescapable mutuality. Therefore, no American can afford to be apathetic about the problem of racial justice. It is a problem that meets every man at his front door.

. . . **Conscience.** I expect that this generation of Negro children throughout the United States will grow up stronger and better because of the courage, the dignity, and the suffering of the nine children of Little Rock, and their counterparts in Nashville, Clinton, and Sturges. And I believe that the white people of this country are being affected too, that beneath the surface this nation's conscience is being stirred.

. . . **Fascism.** If Americans permit thought-control, business-control, and freedom-control to continue, we shall surely move within the shadows of fascism.

. . . **Freedom.** We will reach the goal of freedom in Birmingham and all over the nation, because the goal of America is freedom. Abused and scorned though we may be, our destiny is tied up with America's destiny. Before the pilgrims landed at Plymouth, we were here. Before the pen of Jefferson etched the majestic words of the Declaration of Independence across the pages of history, we were here. For more than two centuries our forebears labored in this country without wages; they made cotton king; they built the homes of their masters while suffering gross injustice and shameful humiliation—and yet out of a bottomless vitality they continued to thrive and develop. If the inexpressible cruelties of slavery could not stop us, the opposition we now face will surely fail. We will win our freedom because the sacred heritage of our nation and the eternal will of God are embodied in our echoing demands.

We could not be where we are today without the great rights of free speech, free press, freedom to demonstrate, petition and march to the seat of Government, even in Montgomery, Alabama, where redress of grievances may be brought.

Throughout the upheavals of cold-war politics, Negroes had seen their government go to the brink of nuclear conflict more than once. The justification for risking the annihiliation of the human race was always expressed in terms of America's willingness to go to any lengths to preserve freedom. To the Negro that readiness for heroic measures in the defense of liberty disappeared or became tragically weak when the threat was within our own borders and was concerned with the Negro's liberty. While the Negro is not so selfish as to stand isolated in concern for his own dilemma, ignoring the ebb and flow of events around the world, there is a certain bitter irony in the picture of his country championing freedom in foreign lands and failing to ensure that freedom to twenty million of its own.

. . . **Free Elections.** The advocacy of free elections in Europe by American officials is hypocrisy when free elections are not held in great sections of America.

. . . **Future.** Any plan for the future, which seeks to calm troubled waters will have to sweep barriers away, rather than pour oil over turbulent tides.

. . . **Militarism.** A nation that continues year after year to

3

spend more money on military defense than on programs of social uplift is approaching its spiritual death.

. . . **Morality.** America, I wonder whether your moral and spiritual progress has been commensurate with your scientific progress. It appears to me that your moral progress lags behind your scientific progress, your mentality outdistances your morality, and your civilization outshines your culture.

. . . **Prejudice.** The strands of prejudice toward Negroes are tightly wound around the American character.

. . . **Progress.** It is, in point historical measurement, only a flicker of an eye since a labor union was, in this country, a criminal conspiracy, a Negro a chattel, a pacifist an anarchist, and any aggressive disciple of the theory of the redistribution of wealth a dangerous radical.

. . . **Race Problem.** History has thrust upon our generation an indescribably important destiny—to complete a process of democratization which our nation has too long developed too slowly, but which is our most powerful weapon for world respect and emulation. How we deal with this crucial situation (race problem) will determine our moral health as individuals, our cultural health as a region, our political health as a nation, and our prestige as a leader of the free world. The future of America is bound up with the solution of the present crisis.

The racial problem will be solved in America to the degree that every American considers himself personally confronted with it. Whether one lives in the heart of the Deep South or on the periphery of the North, the problem of injustice is his problem; it is his problem because it is America's problem.

The shape of the world today does not permit us the luxury of a faltering democracy. The United States cannot hope to attain the respect of the vital and growing colored nations of the world unless it remedies its racial problems at home.

. . . **Racism.** Our nation was born in genocide when it embraced the doctrine that the original American, the Indian, was an inferior race. Even before there were large numbers of

Negroes on our shores, the scar of racial hatred had already disfigured colonial society. From the sixteenth century forward, blood flowed in battles over racial supremacy. We are perhaps the only nation which tried as a matter of national policy to wipe out its indigenous population. Moreover, we elevated that tragic experience into a noble crusade. Indeed, even today we have not permitted ourselves to reject or to feel remorse for this shameful episode. Our literature, our films, our drama, our folklore all exalt it.

Ever since the signing of the Declaration of Independence, America has manifested a schizophrenic personality on the question of race. She has been torn between selves—a self in which she has proudly professed democracy and a self in which she has sadly practiced the antithesis of democracy.

For too long the depth of racism in American life has been underestimated. The surgery to extract it is necessarily complex and detailed. As a beginning it is important to X-ray our history and reveal the full extent of the disease.

. . . **Tradition of Violence.** Acceptance of nonviolent direct action was a proof of a certain sophistication on the part of the Negro masses; for it showed that they dared to break with the old, ingrained concepts of our society. The eye-for-an-eye philosophy, the impulse to defend oneself when attacked, has always been held as the highest measure of American manhood. We are a nation that worships the frontier tradition, and our heroes are those who champion justice through violent retaliation against injustice. It is not simple to adopt the credo that moral force has as much strength and virtue as the capacity to return a physical blow; or that to refrain from hitting back requires more will and bravery than the automatic reflexes of defense.

. . . **Unity.** The racial issue that we confront in America is not a sectional but a national problem. The citizenship rights of Negroes cannot be flouted anywhere without impairing the rights of every other American. Injustice anywhere is a threat to justice everywhere. A breakdown of law in Alabama weakens the very foundations of lawful government in the other fifty states.

5

. . . **World Opinion.** Oxford, Mississippi, has placed democracy on trial. As never before, the cry of the Negro for equality and justice in our nation has been muffled, at best. But the Little Rocks, the Montgomerys, the Albanys and the Oxfords place the questioning of our world leadership on the lips of the emerging African and Asian nations. We cannot stand before the judgment bar of world opinion so long as there erupts an Oxford, Mississippi. What we are doing speaks so loud they cannot hear what we say.

AMERICAN IMAGE

The national government is realizing that our so-called domestic race relations are a major force in our foreign relations. Our image abroad reflects our behavior at home.

APATHY

If the moderates of the white South fail to act now, history will have to record that the greatest tragedy of this period of social transition was not the strident clamor of the bad people, but the appalling silence of the good people. Our generation will have to repent not only for the acts and words of the children of darkness but also for the fears and apathy of the children of light.

The ultimate tragedy of Birmingham was not the brutality of the bad people, but the silence of the good people.

ARMAMENT

. . . **Church.** The church cannot be silent while mankind faces the threat of nuclear annihilation. If the church is true to her mission, she must call for an end to the arms race.

. . . **Fear.** The nations have believed that greater armaments will cast out fear. But alas! they have produced greater fear.

·· B ··

BIBLE

. . . **Misinterpretation.** There is always the danger that religion and the Bible not properly interpreted can be used as forces to crystallize the status quo.

BIRMINGHAM

The masses of white citizens in Birmingham were not fighting us. This was one of the most amazing aspects of the Birmingham crusade. Only a year or so ago, had we begun such a campaign, Bull Connor would have had his job done for him by murderously angry white citizens. Now, however, the majority were maintaining a strictly hands-off policy. I do not mean to insinuate that they were in sympathy with our cause or that they boycotted stores because we did. I simply suggest that it is powerfully symbolic of shifting attitudes in the South that the majority of the white citizens of Birmingham remained neutral through our campaign. This neutrality added force to our feeling that we were on the road to victory.

. . . **Children.** The introduction of Birmingham's children into the (civil rights) campaign was one of the wisest moves we made. It brought a new impact to the crusade, and the impetus that we needed to win the struggle.

. . . **Civil Disobedience.** When the injunction (against Negro demonstrations) was issued in Birmingham, our failure to obey it bewildered our opponents. They did not know what to do. We did not hide our intentions. In fact, I announced our plan to the press, pointing out that we were not anarchists advocating lawlessness, but that it was obvious to us that the courts of Alabama had misused the judicial process in order to perpetuate injustice and segregation. Consequently, we could not, in good conscience, obey their findings.

BITTERNESS

When a man walks the streets day in and day out with no job, when a man sees life as a long and desolate corridor with no exit sign, it sometimes is difficult for him to hear ideas of nonviolence. He develops a bitterness toward life and toward society.

BLACK MUSLIMS

Most of those to whom the Muslims appealed were in fact expressing resentment for the lack of militancy which had long prevailed in the freedom movement. When the Negroes' fighting spirit soared in the summer of 1963, the appeal of the Muslims declined precipitously. Today, as I travel throughout the country, I am struck by how few American Negroes (except in a handful of big-city ghettos) have even heard of the Muslim movement, much less given allegiance to its pessimistic doctrine.

(There is a) force . . . of bitterness and hatred, and it comes perilously close to advocating violence. It is expressed in the various black nationalist groups that are springing up across the nation, the largest and best-known being Elijah Muhammad's Muslim movement. Nourished by the Negro's frustration over the continued existence of racial discrimination, this movement is made up of people who have lost faith in America, who have absolutely repudiated Christianity, and who have concluded that the white man is an incorrigible "devil."

BLACK POWER

Once a helpless child, the Negro has now grown politically, culturally, and economically. Many white men fear retaliation. The Negro must show them that they have nothing to fear, for the Negro forgives and is willing to forget the past. *The Negro must convince the white man that he seeks justice for both himself and the white man.* A mass movement exercising love and nonviolence and demonstrating power under discipline should convince the white community that were such a movement to attain strength, its power would be used creatively and not vengefully.

A guilt-ridden white minority lives in fear that if the Negro should ever attain power, he would act without restraint or pity to revenge the injustices and brutality of the years. It is something like a parent who continually mistreats a son. One day that parent raises his hand to strike the son, only to discover that the son is now as tall as he is. The parent is suddenly afraid—fearful that the son will use his new physical power to repay his parent for all the blows of the past.

Through nonviolence we avoid the temptation of taking on the psychology of victors. Thanks largely to the noble and invaluable work of the NAACP, we have won great victories in the federal courts. But we must not be self-satisfied. We must respond to every decision with an understanding of those who have opposed us, and with acceptance of the new adjustments that the court orders pose for them. We must act in such a way that our victories will be triumphs for good will in all men, white and Negro.

. . . **And White Backlash.** It is a false assumption that so-called white backlash is caused by the slogan, "black power." Actually the black power slogan has been exploited by the decision makers to justify resistance to change.

BOYCOTTS

When I urged that concept of selective buying or economic withdrawal be utilized to speed the end of Alabama's cradle to the grave system of segregation, I found a hesitation among many men of good will. The principle was questioned. Some suggest it was alien, or foreign in principle. Let me assure you that it is as American and as effective as that famous cry, "No taxation without representation."

As we struggle for freedom in America we will have to boycott at times. But we must remember, as we do so, that a boycott is not an end itself; it is merely a means to awaken a sense of shame within the oppressor and challenge his false sense of superiority. The end is reconciliation; the end is redemption; the end is the creation of the beloved community.

The boycott method could be used to unethical and unchristian ends. . . . A boycott suggests an economic squeeze, leaving one bogged down in a negative. But we were concerned (in Montgomery) with the positive. Our concern would not be to put the bus company out of business, but to put justice in business.

BROTHERHOOD

All humanity is involved in a single process, and all men are brothers. To the degree that I harm my brother, no matter what he is doing to me, to that extent I am harming myself. For example, white men often refuse federal aid to education in order to avoid giving the Negro his rights; but because all men are brothers they cannot deny Negro children without harming their own. They end, all efforts to the contrary, by hurting themselves. Why is this? Because men are brothers. If you harm me, you harm yourself.

I refuse to accept the idea that man is mere flotsam and jetsam in the river of life which surrounds him. I refuse to accept the view that mankind is so tragically bound to the starless midnight of racism and war that the bright daybreak of peace and brotherhood can never become a reality.

Through our scientific genuis we have made of the world a neighborhood; now through our moral and spiritual genuis we must make of it a brotherhood.

The agony of the poor diminishes the rich, and the salvation of the weak enriches the strong; we are inevitably our brother's keeper because of the interrelated structure of reality.

Centuries ago, civilization acquired the certain knowledge that man had emerged from barbarity only to the degree that he recognized his relatedness to his fellow man.

·· C ··

CAPITALISM

. . . **Weakness.** In the face of the Communist challenge we must examine honestly the weaknesses of traditional capitalism. In all fairness, we must admit that capitalism has often left a gulf between superfluous wealth and abject poverty, has created conditions permitting necessities to be taken from the many to give luxuries to the few, and has encouraged small-hearted men to become cold and conscienceless so that, like Dives before Lazarus, they are unmoved by suffering, poverty-stricken humanity.

CHANGE

The softminded man always fears change. He feels security in the status quo, and he has an almost morbid fear of the new. For him, the greatest pain is the pain of a new idea. An elderly segregationist in the South is reported to have said, "I have come to see now that desegregation is inevitable. But I pray God that it will not take place until after I die." The soft-minded person always wants to freeze the moment and hold life in the gripping yoke of sameness.

Change is not accomplished by peeling off superficial layers when the causes are rooted deeply in the heart of the organism.

. . . **Resistance.** I would not wish to give the impression that nonviolence will accomplish miracles overnight. Men are not easily moved from their mental ruts or purged of their prejudices and irrational feelings. When the underprivileged demand freedom, the privileged at first react with bitterness and resistance. Even when the demands are couched in terms, the initial response is substantially the same.

CHAUVINISM

One of the great tragedies of man's long trek along the highway of history has been the limiting of neighborly concern to tribe, race, class, or nation. The God of early Old Testament days was a tribal god and the ethic was tribal. "Thou shalt not kill" meant "Thou shalt not kill a fellow Israelite, but for God's sake, kill a Philistine." Greek democracy embraced a certain aristocracy, but not the hordes of Greek slaves whose labors built the city-states. The universalism at the center of the Declaration of Independence has been shamefully negated by America's appalling tendency to substitute "some" for "all."

CHICAGO

. . . **Slums.** Chicago is the capital of segregation in the North; transformation of its slums will leave no northern city secure with its own.

CHRIST

Too often . . . men have responded to Christ emotionally, but they have not responded to his teachings morally. The notion of a personal Savior who has died for us has a great deal of appeal, but too often Christians tend to see the Resurrected Christ, and ignore the man Jesus, turning His face to Jerusalem and deliberately accepting crucifixion rather than deny God's will and give in to the pressures of the Scribes and Pharisees to take back much of what He had taught concerning all men as sons of God.

CHRISTIANITY

The Christian gospel is a two-way road. On the one hand it seeks to change the souls of men, and thereby unite them with God; on the other hand it seeks to change the environmental conditions of men so that the soul will have a chance after it is changed.

The Christian faith makes it possible for us nobly to accept that which cannot be changed, to meet disappointments and sorrow with an inner poise, and to absorb the most intense pain without abandoning our sense of hope.

. . . **Good and Evil.** Christianity clearly affirms that in the long struggle between good and evil, good eventually will emerge as victor. Evil is ultimately doomed by the powerful, inexorable forces of good. Good Friday must give way to the triumphant music of Easter. Degrading tares choke the sprouting necks of growing wheat for a season, but when the harvest is gleaned the evil tares will be separated from the good wheat. Caesar occupied a palace and Christ a cross, but the same Christ so split history into A.D. and B.C. that even the reign of Caesar was subsequently dated by his name.

. . . **Unity.** The broad universalism standing at the center of the gospel makes both the theory and practice of racial injustice morally unjustifiable. Racial prejudice is a blatant denial of the unity which we have in Christ, for in Christ there is neither Jew nor Gentile, bond nor free, Negro nor white.

CHRISTIANS

Every true Christian is a citizen of two worlds, the world of time and the world of eternity.

. . . **Nonconformity.** We as Christians have a mandate to be nonconformists. . . . We are called to be people of conviction, not conformity; of moral nobility, not social respectability. We are commanded to live differently and according to a higher loyalty.

CHURCH

If the church does not participate actively in the struggle for peace and for economic and racial justice, it will forfeit the loyalty of millions and cause men everywhere to say that it has atrophied its will. But if the church will free itself from the shackles of a deadening status quo, and, recovering its great historic mission, will speak and act fearlessly and insistently in terms of justice and peace, it will enkindle the imagination of mankind and fire the souls of men, imbuing them with a glowing and ardent love for truth, justice, and peace.

The erstwhile sanction by the church of slavery, racial segregation, war, and economic exploitation is testimony to the fact that the church has hearkened more to the authority of the world than to the authority of God. Called to be the moral guardian of the community, the church at times has preserved that which is immoral and unethical. Called to combat social evils, it has remained silent behind stained-glass windows. Called to lead men on the highway of brotherhood and to summon them to rise above the narrow confines of race and class, it has enunciated and practiced racial exclusiveness.

How often the church has been an echo rather than a voice, a taillight behind the Supreme Court and other secular agencies, rather than a headlight guiding men progressively and decisively to higher levels of understanding.

In the midst of blatant injustices inflicted upon the Negro, I have watched white churchmen stand on the sideline and mouth pious irrelevancies and sanctimonious trivialities. In the midst of a mighty struggle to rid our nation of racial and economic injustice, I have heard many ministers say: "Those are social issues, with which the gospel has no real concern." And I have watched many churches commit themselves to a completely otherwordly religion which makes a strange, un-Biblical distinction between body and soul, between the sacred and the secular.

The Greek Church in Russia allied itself with the status quo and became so inextricably bound to the despotic czarist regime that it became impossible to be rid of the corrupt political and social system without being rid of the church. Such is the fate of every ecclesiastical organization that allies itself with things-as-they-are.

Millions of people do feel that the church provides an answer to the deep confusion that encompasses their lives. It is still the one familiar landmark where the weary traveler by midnight comes. It is the one house which stands where it has always stood, the house to which the man traveling at midnight either comes or refuses to come. Some decide not to come. But many who come and knock are desperately seeking a little bread to tide them over.

If the church of today does not recapture the sacrificial spirit of the early church, it will lose its authentic right, forfeit the loyalty of millions, and be dismissed as an irrelevant social club with no meaning for the twentieth century.

Gradually . . . the church became so entrenched in wealth and prestige that it began to dilute the strong demands of the gospel and to conform to the ways of the world. And ever since the church has been a weak and ineffectual trumpet making uncertain sounds.

. . . **Action.** There was a time when the church was very powerful—in the time when the early Christians rejoiced at being deemed worthy to suffer for what they believed. In those days the church was not merely a thermometer that recorded the ideas and principles of popular opinion; it was a thermostat that transformed the mores of society.

. . . **Civil Rights.** The church must become increasingly active in social action outside its doors. It must seek to keep channels of communication open between the Negro and white community. It must take an active stand against the injustice that Negroes confront in housing, education, police protection, and in city and state courts. It must exert its influence in the area of economic justice. As guardian of the moral and spiritual life of the community the church cannot look with indifference upon these glaring evils.

. . . **Defender of Status Quo.** The contemporary church is so often a weak, ineffectual voice with an uncertain sound. It is so often the arch supporter of the status quo. Far from being disturbed by the presence of the church, the power structure of the average community is consoled by the church's often vocal sanction of things as they are.

. . . **Early Christian.** We need to recapture the gospel glow of the early Christians, who were nonconformists in the truest sense of the word and refused to shape their witness according to the mundane patterns of the world. Willingly they sacrificed fame, fortune, and life itself in behalf of a cause they knew to be right. Quantitatively small, they were qualitatively giants.

. . . **Negro.** Two types of Negro churches have failed. . . . One burns with emotionalism, and the other freezes with classicism. The former, reducing worship to entertainment, places more emphasis on volume than on content and confuses spirituality with muscularity. The danger in such a church is that the members may have more religion in the hands and feet than in their hearts and souls. . . . The other type of Negro church . . . has developed a class system and boasts of its dignity, its membership of professional people, and its exclusiveness. In such a church the worship service is cold and meaningless, the music dull and uninspiring, and the sermon little more than a homily on current events.

. . . **Racism.** The wedding of Christ with the culture of the South may well prove to be the end of Christianity as a world religion. For these churches, by some strange trick of fate, were the ones that did much of the missionary work in Africa and Asia. It is no coincidence that missionaries are no longer welcome in many of these countries as they attain their freedom. Though missionaries did contribute to the health and education of the people of these countries, the Bread of Life was baked with the bitter leaven of racism within and it is now being spewed out of the mouths of new African leaders who see it as part of a colonialist conspiracy to enslave God's black children.

. . . **Responsibility.** It has always been the responsibility of the church to broaden horizons, challenge the status quo, and break the mores when necessary. The task of conquering segregation is an inescapable *must* confronting the church today.

. . . **Segregation.** One of the shameful tragedies of history is that the very institution (the church) which should remove man from the midnight of racial segregation participates in creating and perpetuating the midnight.

Many segregationists are now retreating to the church as a last refuge for their possible control and influence. They are becoming resigned to the fact that the public sector of life will be integrated by the order of the courts and Congress. This leaves the church as one area which cannot come under court order, where they still might perpetuate their sickness and bitterness against the Negro.

If church people would accept the justice of open occupancy, segregation in housing would completely disappear in a matter of a few years.

It will be one of the tragedies of Christian history if future historians record that at the height of the twentieth century the church was one of the greatest bulwarks of white supremacy.

We must face the shameful fact that the church is the most segregated major institution in American society, and the most segregated hour of the week is, as Professor Liston Pope has pointed out, eleven o'clock on Sunday morning. How often the church has been an echo rather than a voice, a taillight behind the Supreme Court and other secular agencies, rather than a headlight guiding men progressively and decisively to higher levels of understanding.

Christians marched with us in Albany, Georgia, and were accompanied by Jewish rabbis; they rode buses with us in the Freedom Rides; but still many returned to churches and synagogues whose congregations were disturbed that a Negro was about to move into their neighborhoods. Nothing more vividly illustrates the dilemma of the church.

. . . **Social Action.** It is not enough for the church to be active in the realm of ideas; it must move out into the arena of social action.

. . . **Social Concern.** The church is challenged to make the gospel of Jesus Christ relevant within the social situation. We must come to see the Christian gospel as a two-way road. On the one side, it seeks to change the souls of men and thereby unite them with God; on the other, it seeks to change the environmental conditions of men so that the soul will have a chance after it is changed. Any religion that professes to be concerned with the souls of men and yet is not concerned with the economic and social conditions that strangle them and the social conditions that cripple them is the kind the Marxist describes as "an opiate of the people."

. . . **Social Responsibility.** In spite of the noble affirmations of Christianity, the church has often lagged in its concern for social justice and too often has been content to mouth pious irrelevancies and sanctimonious trivialities. It has often been so absorbed in a future good "over yonder" that it forgets the present evils "down here."

Colonialism could not have been perpetuated if the Christian Church had really taken a stand against it. One of the chief defenders of the vicious system of apartheid in South Africa today is the Dutch Reformed Protestant Church. In America slavery could not have existed for almost two hundred and fifty years if the church had not sanctioned it, nor could segregation discrimination exist today if the Christian Church were not a silent and often vocal partner.

. . . **South.** If ever the white ministers of the South decide to declare in a united voice the truth of the gospel on the question of race, the transition from a segregated to an integrated society will be infinitely smoother.

If the church in the South would stand up for the Rights of Negroes, there would be no murder and brutality. The awful fact about the South is that Southerners are making the Marxist anaysis of history more accurate than the Christian hope that men can be persuaded through teaching and preaching to live a new and better life. In the South, businessmen act much more quickly from economic considerations than do churchmen from moral considerations.

. . . **Unity.** The church is the Body of Christ. When the church is true to its nature, it knows neither division nor disunity.

. . . **War.** What more pathetically reveals the irrelevancy of the church in present-day world affairs than its witness regarding war? In a world gone mad with arms buildups, chauvinistic passions, and imperialistic exploitation, the church has either endorsed these activities or remained appallingly silent. During the last two world wars, national churches even functioned as the ready lackeys of the state, sprinkling holy water upon the battleships and joining the mighty armies in singing, "Praise the Lord and pass the ammunition." A weary world, pleading desperately for peace, has often found the church morally sanctioning war.

CHURCH AND STATE

The church must be reminded that it is not the master or the servant of the state, but rather the conscience of the state. It must be the guide and the critic of the state, and never its tool. If the church does not recapture its prophetic zeal, it will become an irrelevant social club without moral or spiritual authority.

CITIZENS COUNCILS

. . . Violence. The Citizens Councils often argue piously that they abhor violence, but their defiance of the law, their unethical methods, and their vitriolic public pronouncements inevitably create the atmosphere in which violence thrives.

CIVIL DISOBEDIENCE

If any earthly institution or custom conflicts with God's will, it is your Christian duty to oppose it.

In no sense do I advocate evading or defying the law as the rabid segregationist would do. This would lead to anarchy. One who breaks an unjust law must do so *openly, lovingly* . . . and with a willingness to accept the penalty.

I don't think any society can call an individual irresponsible who breaks a law and willingly accepts the penalty, if conscience tells him that that law is unjust. I think that this is a long tradition in our society, it is a long tradition in Biblical history.

Civil disobedience can never be legal. These would certainly be contradictory terms. In fact, civil disobedience means that it is not legal. . . . The determining factor is willingness to accept penalties.

Ordinarily, a person leaving a courtroom with a conviction behind him would wear a somber face. But I left with a smile. I knew that I was a convicted criminal (convicted of violating the Alabama anti-boycott law during the Montgomery bus boycott), but I was proud of my crime. It was the crime of joining my people in a nonviolent protest against injustice. It was the crime of seeking to instill within my people a sense of dignity and self-respect. It was the crime of desiring for my people the unalienable rights of life, liberty, and the pursuit of happiness.

There is nothing new about . . . civil disobedience. It was seen sublimely in the refusal of Shadrach, Meshach, and Abednego to obey the laws of Nebuchadnezzar because a higher moral law was involved. It was practiced superbly by the early Christians, who were willing to face hungry lions and the excruciating pain of chopping blocks before submitting to certain unjust laws of the Roman Empire. To a degree, academic freedom is a reality today because Socrates practiced civil disobedience.

Wherever unjust laws exist people on the basis of conscience have a right to disobey those laws.

He who openly disobeys a law, a law that conscience tells him is unjust, and then willingly accepts the penalty, gives evidence thereby that he so respects that law that he belongs in jail until it is changed. Our appeal is to the conscience.

We should remember that everything Adolf Hitler did in Germany was "legal" and everything the Hungarian freedom fighters did in Hungary was "illegal." It was "illegal" to aid and comfort a Jew in Hitler's Germany. Even so, I am sure that, had I lived in Germany at the time, I would have aided and comforted my Jewish brothers. If today I lived in a Communist country where certain principles dear to the Christian faith are suppressed, I would openly advocate disobeying that country's antireligious laws.

There is nothing that expressed massive civil disobedience

any more than the Boston Tea Party, and yet we give this to our young people and our students as a part of the great tradition of our nation. So I think we are in good company when we break unjust laws, and I think those who are willing to do it and accept the penalty are those who are part of the saving of the nation.

CIVIL RIGHTS

In a sense, the well-meaning or the ill-meaning American who asks: "What more will the Negro want?" or "When will he be satisfied?" or "What will it take to make these demonstrations cease?" is asking the Negro to purchase something that already belongs to him by every concept of law, justice and our Judaeo-Christian heritage. Moreover, he is asking the Negro to accept half the loaf and to pay for that half by waiting willingly for the other half to be distributed in crumbs over a hard and protracted winter of injustice. I would like to ask those people who seek to apportion to us the rights they have always enjoyed whether they believe that the framers of the Declaration of Independence intended that liberty should be divided into installments, doled out on a deferred-payment plan. Did not nature create birth as a single process? Is not freedom the negation of servitude? Does not one have to end totally for the other to begin?

There is a terrible parallel between the outstretched and greedy hand of a slave trafficker who sold a Negro his own person, and the uplifted and admonishing finger of people who say today: "What more will the Negro expect if he gains such rights as integrated schools, public facilities, voting rights and progress in housing? Will he, like Oliver Twist, demand more?"

If the executive and legislative branches were as concerned about the protection of the citizenship rights of all people as the federal courts have been, the transition from a segregated to an integrated society would be much further along than it is today. The dearth of positive leadership from Washington is not confined to one political party. Both major parties have lagged in the service of justice. Many Democrats have betrayed it by capitulating to the undemocratic practices of the Southern Dixiecrats. Many Republicans have betrayed it by capitulating to the hypocrisy of right-wing Northerners.

The logic of growth means that the civil rights odyssey must move to new levels in which the content of freedom is security, opportunity, culture and equal participation in the political process.

The quality and quantity of discrimination and deprivation in our nation are so pervasive that all the changes of a decade merely initiated preliminary alterations in an edifice of injustice and misery. But the evils in our society oppressing the Negro are not now so heavy a social and moral burden that white America cannot still live with them. That is the dilemma . . . for which the white leadership has no clear and effective policy.

If the Negro is still saying, "Not enough," it is because he does not feel that he should be expected to be *grateful* for the halting and inadequate attempts of his society to catch up with the basic rights he ought to have inherited automatically, centuries ago, by virtue of his membership in the human family and his American birthright.

Those whites without a vested interest in segregation have found acceptable exactly the changes that the nonviolent demonstrations present as their central demands. Those objectives Negroes have dramatized, fought for and defined have clearly become fair and reasonable demands to the white population, both North and South.

The sooner our society admits that the Negro Revolution is no momentary outburst soon to subside into placid passivity, the easier the future will be for us all.

. . . **Brotherhood.** The Negro in winning rights for himself produces substantial benefits for the nation. Just as a doctor will occasionally reopen a wound, because a dangerous infection hovers beneath the half-healed surface, the revolution for human rights is opening up unhealthy areas in American life and permitting a new and wholesome healing to take place. Eventually the civil rights movement will have contributed infinitely more to the nation than the eradication of racial injustice. It will have enlarged the concept of brotherhood to a vision of total interrelatedness.

. . . **Delayed.** For years now I have heard the word "wait." It rings in the ear of every Negro with a piercing familiarity. This "wait" has almost always meant "never." It has been a tranquilizing thalidomide, relieving the emotional stress for a moment, only to give birth to an all-formed infant of frustration.

. . . **Moderation.** If moderation means pressing on for justice with wise restraint and calm reasonableness, then it is a virtue which all must seek to achieve in this tense period of transition. But if moderation means slowing up in the move toward freedom and capitulating to the whims and caprices of the guardians of a deadening status quo, then moderation is a tragic vice which all men of good will must condemn.

. . . **Morality.** Freedom and justice are ethical demands of the universe. America's motive for giving the Negro freedom must not be merely to compete with godless Communism. It must be done, in the final analysis, not because it is diplomatically expedient but because it is morally compelling.

. . . **Opposition.** Negroes have benefited from a limited change that was emotionally satisfying but materially deficient. As they move forward for fundamental alteration of their lives, a more bitter opposition grows even within groups that were hospitable to earlier superficial amelioration. Conflicts are unavoidable because a stage has been reached in which the reality of equality will require extensive adjustments in the way of life of some of the white majority.

CIVIL RIGHTS AND LABOR

In the case of organized labor, an alliance with the Negro civil rights movement is not a matter of choice but a necessity. If Negroes have almost no rights in the South, labor has few more; if Negroes have inadequate political influence in Congress, labor is barely better off; if automation is a threat to Negroes, it is equally a menace to organized labor.

CIVIL RIGHTS MOVEMENT

The (race) crisis developed when the collective pressures to achieve fair goals for the Negro met with tenacious and determined resistance. Then the emerging new order, based on the principle of democratic equalitarianism, came face to face with the older order, based on the principles of paternalism and subordination. The crisis was not produced by outside agitators, NAACP'ers, Montgomery Protestors, or even the Supreme Court. The crisis developed, paradoxically, when the most sublime principles of American democracy—imperfectly realized for almost two centuries—began fulfilling themselves and met with the brutal resistance of forces seeking to contract and repress freedom's growth.

In this (Negro) revolution no plans have been written for retreat. Those who will not get into step will find that the parade has passed them by.

This (Negro) revolution is genuine because it was born from the same womb that always gives birth to massive social upheavals—the womb of intolerable conditions and unendurable situations. In this time and circumstance, no leader or set of leaders could have acted as ringmasters, whipping a whole race out of purring contentment into leonine courage and action. If such credit is to be given to any single group, it might well go to the segregationists, who, with their callous and cynical code, helped to arouse and ignite the righteous wrath of the Negro.

The enemies of racial progress—and even some of its "friends," who are "for it, but not so fast"—would delight in believing that there is chaos up front in the civil rights ranks.

. . . **Strength.** A new stage in civil rights has been reached, which calls for a new policy. What has changed is our strength. The upsurge of power in the civil rights movement has given it greater maneuverability, and substantial security. It is now strong enough to form alliances, to make commitments in exchange for pledges, and if the pledges are unredeemed, it remains powerful enough to walk out without being shattered or weakened.

24

COLONIALISM

The conflict between two determined forces, the colonial powers and the Asian and African peoples, has been one of the most momentous and critical struggles of the twentieth century.

COMMITMENT

A man who won't die for *something* is not fit to live.

No one ever makes a great contribution to humanity without . . . (a) majestic sense of purpose and . . . dogged determination. No one ever brings his potentiality into actuality without . . . (a) powerful inner drive.

We who cannot accept the creed of the Communists recognize their zeal and commitment to a cause which they believe will create a better world. They have a sense of purpose and destiny, and they work passionately and assiduously to win others to Communism. How many Christians are as concerned to win others to Christ?

˙ If a people can produce from its ranks five per cent who will go voluntarily to jail for a just cause, surely nothing can thwart its ultimate triumph.

It is still one of the tragedies of human history that the "children of darkness" are frequently more determined and zealous than the "children of light."

COMMUNICATIONS

A great deal has been said about a dialogue between Negro and white. Genuinely to achieve it requires that all the media of communication open their channels wide.

COMMUNISM

With all of its false assumptions and evil methods, Communism arose as a protest against the injustices and indignities inflicted upon the underprivileged.

Something in the spirit and threat of Communism challenges us. The late Archbishop of Canterbury, William Temple, referred to Communism as a Christian heresy. He meant that Communism had laid hold on certain truths which are essential parts of the Christian view of things, although bound to them are theories and practices which no Christian could ever accept.

Communism is based on ethical relativism and accepts no stable moral absolutes. Right and wrong are relative to the most expedient methods for dealing with class war. Communism exploits the dreadful philosophy that the end justifies the means.

Communism thrives only when the doors of opportunity are closed and human aspirations are stifled.

We should as Christians pray for the Communist constantly, but never can we, as true Christians, tolerate the philosophy of Communism.

The trouble with Communism is that it has neither a theology nor a Christology; therefore it emerges with a mixed-up anthropology. Confused about God, it is also confused about man. In spite of its glowing talk about the welfare of the masses, Communism's methods and philosophy strip man of his dignity and worth, leaving him as little more than a depersonalized cog in the ever-turning wheel of the state.

After our condemnation of the philosophy of Communism has been eloquently expressed, we must with positive action seek to remove those conditions of poverty, insecurity, injustice, and racial discrimination which are the fertile soil in which the seed of Communism grows and develops.

. . . **Atheism.** Communism is based on a materialistic and humanistic view of life and history. According to Communist theory, matter, not mind or spirit, speaks the last word in the universe. Such a philosophy is avowedly secularistic and atheistic. Under it, God is merely a figment of the imagination, religion is a product of fear and ignorance, and the church is an invention of the rulers to control the masses.

. . . **Means and Ends.** Since for the Communist there is no divine government, no absolute moral order, there are no fixed, immutable principles; consequently almost anything—

force, violence, murder, lying—is a justifiable means to the "millennial" end.

COMMUNISM AND CAPITALISM

Truth is not to be found either in traditional capitalism or in Marxism. Each represents a partial truth. Historically, capitalism failed to discern the truth in collective enterprise and Marxism failed to see the truth in individual enterprise. Nineteenth-century capitalism failed to appreciate that life is social, and Marxism failed, and still fails, to see that life is individual and social. The Kingdom of God is neither the thesis of individual enterprise nor the antithesis of collective enterprise, but a synthesis which reconciles the truth of both.

COMMUNISM AND CHRISTIANITY

Communism is the only serious rival to Christianity. Such great world religions as Judaism, Buddhism, Hinduism, and Mohammedanism are possible alternatives to Christianity, but no one conversant with the hard facts of the modern world will deny that Communism is Christianity's more formidable rival.

Communism and Christianity are fundamentally incompatible. A true Christian cannot be a true Communist, for the two philosophies are antithetical and all the dialectics of the logicians cannot reconcile them.

Communism, avowedly secularistic and materialistic, has no place for God. This I could never accept, for as a Christian I believe that there is a creative personal power in this universe who is the ground and essence of all reality—a power that cannot be explained in materialistic terms.

COMMUNISM AND MAN

The ultimate weakness of Communism is that it robs man of that quality which makes him man. Man, says Paul Tillich, is man because he is free. This freedom is expressed through man's capacity to deliberate, decide, and respond. Under Communism, the individual soul is shackled by the chains of conformity; his spirit is bound by the manacles of party allegiance. He is stripped of both conscience and reason.

In Communism the individual ends up in subjection to the state. True, the Marxist would argue that the state is an "interim" reality which is to be eliminated when the classless society emerges; but the state is the end while it lasts, and man only a means to that end. And if any man's so-called rights or liberties stand in the way of that end, they are simply swept aside. His liberties of expression, his freedom to vote, his freedom to listen to what news he likes or to choose his books are all restricted. Man becomes hardly more, in Communism, than a depersonalized cog in the turning wheel of the state.

COMMUNITY

The cross is the eternal expression of the length to which God will go in order to restore broken community. The resurrection is a symbol of God's triumph over all the forces that seek to block community. The Holy Spirit is the continuing community creating reality that moves through history. He who works against community is working against the whole of creation. Therefore, if I respond to hate with a reciprocal hate I do nothing but intensify the cleavage in broken community. I can only close the gap in broken community by meeting hate with love. If I meet hate with hate, I become depersonalized, because creation is so designed that my personality can only be fulfilled in the context of community.

COMPASSION

An expression of pity, devoid of genuine sympathy, leads to a new form of paternalism which no self-respecting person can accept. Dollars possess the potential for helping wounded children of God on life's Jericho Road, but unless those dollars are distributed by compassionate fingers they will enrich neither the giver nor the receiver. . . . Money devoid of love is like salt devoid of savor, good for nothing except to be trodden under the foot of men. True neighborliness requires personal concern.

The hardhearted person lacks the capacity for genuine compassion. He is unmoved by the pains and afflictions of his brothers. He passes unfortunate men every day, but he never really sees them. He gives dollars to a worthwhile charity, but he gives not of his spirit.

CONCERN

In order to live creatively and meaningfully, our self-concern must be wedded to other-concern.

No man has learned to live until he can rise above the narrow confines of his individualistic concerns to the broader concerns of all humanity. Length without breadth is like a self-contained tributary having no outward flow to the ocean. Stagnant, still and stale, it lacks both life and freshness.

CONCERN FOR THE INDIVIDUAL

The confidence that God is mindful of the individual is of tremendous value in dealing with the disease of fear, for it gives us a sense of worth, of belonging, and of at-homeness in the universe.

CONFLICT

The federal government reacts to events more quickly when a situation of conflict cries out for its intervention.

. . . **Good and Evil.** All of the great religions have recognized a tension at the very core of the universe. Hinduism, for instance, calls this tension a conflict between illusion and reality. Zoroastrianism, a conflict between the god of light and the god of darkness; and traditional Judaism and Christianity, a conflict between God and Satan. Each realizes that in the midst of the upward thrust of goodness there is the downward pull of evil.

CONFORMITY

Everybody passionately seeks to be well-adjusted. We must, of course, be well-adjusted if we are to avoid neurotic and schizophrenic personalities, but there are some things in our world to which men of goodwill must be maladjusted. I confess that I never intend to become adjusted to the evils of segregation and the crippling effects of discrimination, to the moral degeneracy of religious bigotry and the corroding effects of narrow sectarianism, to economic conditions that deprive men of work and food, and to the insanities of militarism and the self-defeating effects of physical violence.

Many people fear nothing more terribly than to take a position which stands out sharply and clearly from the prevailing opinion. The tendency of most is to adopt a view that is so ambiguous that it will include everything and so popular that it will include everybody. . . . Not a few men, who cherish lofty and noble ideals, hide them under a bushel for fear of being called different.

We have cultivated a mass mind and have moved from the extreme of rugged individualism to the even greater extreme of rugged collectivism. We are not makers of history; we are made by history.

Numerous decent, wholesome young persons permit themselves to become involved in unwholesome pursuits which they do not personally condone or even enjoy, because they are ashamed to say no when the gang says yes.

When people think about race problems they are too often more concerned with men than with God. The question usually asked is: "What will my friends think if I am too friendly to Negroes or too liberal on the race question?" Men forget to ask: "What will God think?" And so they live in fear because they tend to seek social approval on the horizontal plane rather than spiritual devotion on the vertical plane.

CONSCIENCE

God's unbroken hold on us is something that will never permit us to feel right when we do wrong or to feel natural when we do the unnatural.

Despite man's tendency to live on low and degrading planes, something reminds him that he is not made for that. As he trails in the dust, something reminds him that he is made for the stars. As he makes folly his bedfellow, a nagging inner voice tells him that he is born for eternity.

Seldom has man thoroughly adjusted himself to evil, for in spite of his rationalizations, compromises, and alibis, he knows the "is" is not the "ought" and the actual is not the possible.

We are developing a coalition of conscience, a grand alliance, which will one day bring an end to the evils that have clouded our days and transform dark years into a bright future.

Man was born into barbarism when killing his fellow man was a normal condition of existence. He became endowed with a conscience. And he has now reached the day when violence toward another human being must become as abhorrent as eating another's flesh.

CONSENSUS

A consensus orientation is understandably attractive to a political leader. . . . None of (the great) Presidents fashioned the program which was to mark him as historically great by patiently awaiting a consensus. Instead, each was propelled into action by a mass movement which did not necessarily reflect an overwhelming majority. What the movement lacked in support was less significant than the fact that it had championed the key issue of the hour. . . . *The overwhelming national consensus followed their acts; it did not precede them.*

COURAGE

We must constantly build dykes of courage to hold back the flood of fear.

Courage is an inner resolution to go forward in spite of obstacles and frightening situations; cowardice is a submissive surrender to circumstance. Courage breeds creative self-affirmation; cowardice produces destructive self-abnegation. Courage faces fear and thereby masters it; cowardice represses fear and is thereby mastered by it.

Courageous men never lose the zest for living even though

their life situation is zestless; cowardly men, overwhelmed by the uncertainties of life, lose the will to live.

A generation of young people has come out of decades of shadows to face naked state power; it has lost its fears, and experienced the majestic dignity of a direct struggle for its own liberation.

Forces that threaten to negate life must be challenged by courage, which is the power of life to affirm itself in spite of life's ambiguities. This requires the exercise of a creative will that enables us to hew out a stone of hope from a mountain of despair.

Courage, the determination not to be overwhelmed by any object, however frightful, enables us to stand up to any fear.

Courage takes the fear produced by a definite object into itself and thereby conquers the fear involved.

COURT DECISIONS

. . . **Enforcement.** It is not generally realized that the burden of court decisions such as the Supreme Court decision on school desegregation places the responsibility on the individual Negro who is compelled to bring a suit in order to obtain his rights. In effect, the most impoverished Americans, facing powerfully equipped adversaries, are required to finance and conduct complex litigation that may involve tens of thousands of dollars. . . . To be forced to accumulate resources for legal actions imposes intolerable hardships on the already overburdened.

COWARDICE

Gandhi often said that if cowardice is the only alternative to violence, it is better to fight.

CRIME

Criminality and delinquency are not racial; poverty and ignorance breed crime whatever the racial group may be.

CRISIS

Every crisis has both its dangers and its opportunities. It can spell either salvation or doom.

CROSS

There are some who still find the Cross a stumbling block, others consider it foolishness, but I am more convinced than ever before that it is the power of God unto social and individual salvation.

··D··

DEATH

Death is inevitable. It is a democracy for all of the people, not an aristocracy for some of the people—kings die and beggars die; young men die and old men die; learned men die and ignorant men die. We need not fear it. The God who brought our whirling planet from primal vapor and has led the human pilgrimage for lo these many centuries can most assuredly lead us through death's dark night into the bright daybreak of eternal life. . . . Death is not the ultimate evil; the ultimate evil is to be outside God's love.

Would not this be a strangely irrational universe . . . if death were a blind alley leading the human race into a state of nothingness?

DEMOCRACY

One of the great glories of democracy is the right to protest for right.

DEMOCRACY AND SEGREGATION

The reality of segregation, like slavery, has always had to confront the ideals of democracy and Christianity. Indeed, segregation and discrimination are strange paradoxes in a nation founded on the principle that all men are created equal.

DEMOCRACY AND TOTALITARIANISM

The conflict we witness between totalitarianism and democracy is fundamentally centered in this: Is man a person or a pawn? Is he a cog in the wheel of the state or a free, creative being capable of accepting responsibility? This inquiry is as old as ancient man and as new as the morning newspaper.

DEMONSTRATIONS

Many, especially in the North, argue that the maximum use of legislation, welfare and anti-poverty programs now replaces demonstrations, and that overt and visible protest should now be abandoned. Nothing could prove more erroneous than to demobilize at this point. It was the mass-action movement that engendered the changes of the decade, but the demands which created it are not yet satisfied. Without the will to unity and struggle Negroes would have no strength, and reversal of their successes could be easily effected. The use of creative tensions that broke the barriers of the South will be as indispensable in the North to obtain and extend necessary objectives.

The Negro has many pent-up resentments and latent frustrations, and he must release them. So let him march; let him make prayer pilgrimages to the city hall; let him go on freedom rides—and try to understand why he must do so. If his repressed emotions are not released in nonviolent ways, they will seek expression through violence; this is not a threat but a fact of history.

I have never felt that demonstrations could actually solve the (race) problem. They dramatize the existence of certain social ills that could very easily be ignored if you did not have demonstrations.

In Selma (Alabama), over 3,000 Negroes from all walks of life went to jail, suffered brutality and discomfort, so that the nation could reexamine the voting registration laws—and find them woefully inadequate. We call it doing witness—you would call it testifying—with our bodies.

Through demonstration, Negroes learn that unity and militance have more force than bullets.

Those who have lived under the corrosive humiliation of daily intimidation are imbued by demonstrations with a sense of courage and dignity that strengthens their personalities.

. . . **Marches.** There is nothing more powerful to dramatize a social evil than the tramp, tramp of marching feet.

DIGNITY

It is ultimately more honorable to walk the streets in dignity than to ride the buses in humiliation.

DIRECTION

In analyzing our campaign in Albany, Georgia, we decided that one of the principal mistakes we had made there was to scatter our efforts too widely. We had been so involved in attacking segregation in general that we had failed to direct our protest effectively to any one major facet. We concluded that in hard-core communities a more effective battle could be waged if it was concentrated against one aspect of the evil and intricate system of segregation.

DISAPPOINTMENT

Shattered dreams are a hallmark of our mortal life.

DISARMAMENT

One cannot be concerned just with civil rights. . . . It is very nice to drink milk at an unsegregated lunch counter—but not when there's Strontium 90 in it.

Only disarmament, based on good faith, will make mutual trust a living reality.

DISCRIMINATION

We must depend on religion and education to alter the errors of the heart and mind; but meanwhile it is an immoral act to compel a man to accept injustice until another man's heart is set straight. As the experience of several Northern states has shown, anti-discrimination laws can provide powerful sanctions against this kind of immorality.

DRAFT

The sooner this country does away with the draft, the better off we'll be.

·· E ··

ECONOMIC EXPLOITATION

Many white Americans of good will have never connected bigotry with economic exploitation. They have deplored prejudice, but tolerated or ignored economic injustice. But the Negro knows that these two evils have a malignant kinship.

ECONOMIC INJUSTICE

Philanthropy is commendable, but it must not cause the philanthropist to overlook the circumstances of economic injustice which make philanthropy necessary.

ECONOMIC OPPORTUNITY FOR NEGROES

The Negro today is not struggling for some abstract, vague rights, but for concrete and prompt improvement in his way of life. What will it profit him to be able to send his children to an integrated school if the family income is insufficient to buy them school clothes? What will he gain by being permitted to move to an integrated neighborhood if he cannot afford to do so because he is unemployed or has a low-paying job with no future? . . . Negroes must not only have the right to go into any establishment open to the public, but they must also be absorbed into our economic system in such a manner that they can afford to exercise that right.

EDUCATION

Education and learning have become tools for shaping the future and not devices of privilege for an exclusive few. Behind this spiritual explosion is the shattering of a material atom.

EDUCATION AND LEGISLATION

Through education we seek to change attitudes; through legislation and court orders we seek to regulate behavior. Through education we seek to change internal feelings (prejudice, hate, etc.); through legislation and court orders we seek to control the external effects of those feelings. Through education we seek to break down the spiritual barriers to integration; through legislation and court orders we seek to break down the physical barriers to integration. One method is not a substitute for the other, but a meaningful and necessary supplement.

ENEMIES

When we look beneath the surface . . . we see within our enemy-neighbor a measure of goodness and know that the viciousness and evilness of his acts are not quite representative of all that he is. We see him in a new light. We recognize that his hate grows out of fear, pride, ignorance, prejudice, and misunderstanding, but in spite of this, we know God's image is ineffably etched in his being. Then we love our enemies by realizing that they are not totally bad.

At times we are able to humiliate our worst enemy. Inevitably, his weak moments come and we are able to thrust in his side the spear of defeat. But this we must not do. Every word and deed must contribute to an understanding with the enemy and release those vast reservoirs of goodwill which have been blocked by impenetrable walls of hate.

EVIL

It is evil that the nonviolent resister seeks to defeat, not the persons victimized by evil.

He who passively accepts evil is as much involved in it as he who helps to perpetrate it. He who accepts evil without protesting against it is really cooperating with it.

Evil carries the seed of its own destruction. In the long run right defeated is stronger than evil triumphant.

Christianity has never dismissed evil as illusory, or an error of the mortal mind. It reckons with evil as a force that has objective reality. But Christianity contends that evil contains the seed of its own destruction. History is the story of evil forces that advance with seemingly irresistible power only to be crushed by the battling rams of the forces of justice.

Evil has a self-defeating quality. It can go a long way, but then it reaches its limit. There is something in this universe that Greek mythology referred to as the goddess of Nemesis.

. . . **Reality.** We may debate the origin of evil, but only a victim of superficial optimism would debate its reality. Evil is stark, grim, and colossally real.

. . . **Resistance.** Evil is recalcitrant and determined, and never voluntarily relinquishes its hold short of a persistent, almost fanatical resistance.

Noncooperation with evil is as much a moral obligation as the cooperation with good.

EXCELLENCE

In the new age, we Negroes will be forced to compete with people of all races and nationalities. Therefore, we cannot aim merely to be good Negro teachers, good Negro doctors, good Negro ministers, good Negro skilled laborers. We must set out to do a good job, irrespective of race, and do it so well that nobody could do it better.

If it falls your lot to be a street-sweeper, sweep streets as Raphael painted pictures, sweep streets as Michelangelo carved marble, sweep streets as Beethoven composed music, sweep streets as Shakespeare wrote poetry. Sweep streets so well that all the hosts of heaven and earth will have to pause and say, "Here lived a great street-sweeper who swept his job well."

EXISTENTIALISM

History is a series of unreconciled conflicts, and man's existence is filled with anxiety and threatened with meaninglessness. While the ultimate Christian answer is not found in any of these existential assertions, there is much here by which the theologian may describe the true state of man's existence.

. . . **Freedom.** An understanding of the "finite freedom" of man is one of the permanent contributions of existentialism, and its perception of the anxiety and conflict produced in man's personal and social life by the perilous and ambiguous structure of existence is especially meaningful for our time.

EXTREMISM

The conservatives who say, "Let us not move so fast," and the extremists who say, "Let us go out and whip the world," would tell you that they are as far apart as the poles. But there is a striking parallel: They accomplish nothing; for they do not reach the people who have a crying need to be free.

The question is not whether we will be extremists, but what kind of extremists we will be. Will we be extremists for the preservation of injustice or for the extension of justice? In that dramatic scene on Calvary's hill three men were crucified. We must never forget that all three were crucified for the same crime—the crime of extremism. Two were extremists for immorality, and thus fell below their environment. The other, Jesus Christ, was an extremist for love, truth and goodness, and thereby rose above his environment. Perhaps the South, the nation and the world are in dire need of creative extremists.

··F··

FAITH

A positive religious faith does not offer an illusion that we shall be exempt from pain and suffering, nor does it imbue us with the idea that life is a drama of unalloyed comfort and untroubled ease. Rather, it instills us with the inner equilibrium needed to face strains, burdens, and fears that inevitably come, and assures us that the universe is trustworthy and that God is concerned.

Two types of faith in God are clearly set forth in the Scriptures. One may be called the mind's faith, wherein the intellect assents to a belief that God exists. The other may be referred to as the heart's faith, whereby the whole man is involved in a trusting act of self-surrender. To know God, a man must possess this latter type of faith, for the mind's faith is directed toward a theory, but the heart's faith is centered in a Person.

Before the ship of your life reaches its last harbor, there will be long, drawn-out storms, howling and jostling winds, and tempestuous seas that make the heart stand still. If you do not have a deep and patient faith in God, you will be powerless to face the delays, disappointments, and vicissitudes that inevitably come.

Our refusal to be stopped, our "courage to be," our determination to go on "in spite of," reveal the divine image within us. The man who has made this discovery knows that no burden can overwhelm him and no wind of adversity can blow his hope away. He can stand anything that can happen to him.

Faith can give us courage to face the uncertainties of the future. It will give our tired feet new strength as we continue our forward stride toward the city of freedom.

FAMILY

Our most fundamental social unit—the family—is tortured, corrupted, and weakened by economic insufficiency. When a Negro man is inadequately paid, his wife must work to provide the simple necessities for the children. When a mother has to work she does violence to motherhood by depriving her children of her loving guidance and protection; often they are poorly cared for by others or by none—left to roam the streets unsupervised. It is not the Negro alone who is wronged by a disrupted society; many white families are in similar straits.

FATALISM

Fatalism implies that everything is foreordained and inescapable. People who subscribe to this philosophy succumb to an absolute resignation to that which they consider to be their fate and think of themselves as being little more than helpless orphans cast into the terrifying immensities of space. Because they believe that man has no freedom, they seek neither to deliberate nor to make decisions, but rather they wait passively for external forces to decide for them. They never actively seek to change their circumstances, for they believe that all circumstances, as in the Greek tragedies, are controlled by irresistible and foreordained forces.

FEAR

Evil and pain in this conundrum of life are close to each of us, and we do both ourselves and our neighbors a great disservice when we attempt to prove that there is nothing in this world of which we should be frightened.

Envy, jealousy, a lack of self-confidence, a feeling of insecurity, and a haunting sense of inferiority are all rooted in fear. We do not envy people and then fear them; first we fear them and subsequently we become jealous of them. Is there a cure for these annoying fears that pervert our personal lives? Yes, a deep and abiding commitment to the way of love.

We shall never be cured of fear by escapism or repression, for the more we attempt to ignore and repress our fears, the more we multiply our inner conflicts.

There are in the white South millions of people of good will whose voices are yet unheard, whose course is yet unclear, and whose courageous acts are yet unseen. These persons are often silent today because of fear—fear of social, political, and economic reprisals. In the name of God, in the interest of human dignity, and for the cause of democracy these millions are called upon to gird their courage, to speak out, to offer the leadership that is needed.

. . . **Creative.** Fear is the elemental alarm system of the human organism which warns of approaching dangers and without which man could not have survived in either the primitive or modern worlds. Fear, moreover, is a powerfully creative force. Every great invention and intellectual advance represents a desire to escape from some dreaded circumstance or condition. The fear of darkness led to the marvelous advances of medical science. The fear of ignorance was one reason that man built great institutions of learning. The fear of war was one of the forces behind the birth of the United Nations. Angelo Patri has rightly said, "Education consists in being afraid at the right time." If man were to lose his capacity to fear, he would be deprived of his capacity to grow, invent, and create.

. . . **Imagination.** More often than not, fear involves the misuse of the imagination.

. . . **Normal and Abnormal.** Abnormal fears are emotionally ruinous and psychologically destructive. To illustrate the difference between normal and abnormal fear, Sigmund Freud spoke of a person who was quite properly afraid of snakes in the heart of an African jungle and of another person who neurotically feared that snakes were under the carpet in his city apartment. Psychologists say that normal children are born with only two fears—the fear of falling and the fear of loud noises—and that all others are environmentally acquired. Most of these acquired fears are snakes under the carpet.

FEAR AND FAITH

Abnormal fears and phobias that are expressed in neurotic anxiety may be cured by psychiatry; but the fear of death, nonbeing, and nothingness, expressed existential anxiety, may be cured only by a positive religious faith.

Our trouble is simply that we attempt to confront fear without faith; we sail through the stormy seas of life without adequate spiritual boats.

FELLOWSHIP

Words cannot express the exultation felt by the individual as he finds himself, with hundreds of his fellows, behind prison bars for a cause he knows is just.

FOREIGN AID

We must use our vast resources of wealth to aid the undeveloped countries of the world. Have we spent far too much of our national budget in establishing military bases around the world and far too little in establishing bases of genuine concern and understanding?

FORGIVENESS

Forgiveness is not an occasional act; it is a permanent attitude.

He who is devoid of the power to forgive is devoid of the power to love.

Forgiveness does not mean ignoring what has been done or putting a false label on an evil act. It means, rather, that the evil act no longer remains as a barrier to the relationship. Forgiveness is a catalyst creating the atmosphere necessary for a fresh start and a new beginning. It is the lifting of a burden or the canceling of a debt.

We can never say, "I will forgive you, but I won't have anything further to do with you." Forgiveness means reconciliation, a coming together again.

FREEDOM

An abiding expression of man's higher spiritual nature is his freedom. Man is man because he is free to operate within the framework of his destiny. He is free to deliberate, to make decisions, and to choose between alternatives. He is distinguished from animals by his freedom to do evil or to do good and to walk the high road of beauty or tread the low road of ugly degeneracy.

Freedom has always been an expensive thing. History is a fit testimony to the fact that freedom is rarely gained without sacrifice and self-denial.

There is nothing in all the world greater than freedom. It it worth paying for; it is worth losing a job for; it is worth going to jail for. I would rather be a free pauper than a rich slave. I would rather die in abject poverty with my convictions than live in inordinate riches with the lack of self-respect.

The forces of both history and Providence are on the side of freedom.

It is no more possible to be half free than it is to be half alive.

Freedom is never voluntarily given by the oppressor; it must be demanded by the oppressed.

. . . **Price.** Callous indifference to human suffering exists to this day, when people who consider themselves men of good will are still asking: "What is the Negro willing to pay if we give him his freedom?"

. . . **Responsibility.** Ask a prisoner released after years of confinement in jail what efforts he faces in taking on the privileges and responsibilities of freedom, and the enormity of the Negroes' task in the years ahead becomes clear.

FREEDOM AND DESTINY

Freedom is always within the framework of destiny. *But there is freedom.* We are both free and destined. Freedom is the act of deliberating, deciding, and responding within our destined nature. Even though destiny may prevent our going to some attractive Spain, we do have the capacity to accept such a disappointment, to respond to it, and to do something about the disappointment itself.

FREEDOM MOVEMENT

The march of freedom is backed up by so many forces that it ultimately cannot be defeated.

It is the obligation of government to move resolutely to the side of the freedom movement. There is a right and a wrong side in this conflict and the government does not belong in the middle.

. . . **Children.** Once when we sent out a call for volunteers, six tiny youngsters responded. Andy Young told them that they were not old enough to go to jail but that they could go to the library. "You won't get arrested there," he said, "but you might learn something." So these six small children marched off to the building in the white district, where, up to two weeks before, they would have been turned away at the door. Shyly but doggedly, they went to the children's room and sat down, and soon they were lost in their books. In their own way, they had struck a blow for freedom.

FREEDOM NOW

It is because the Negro knows that no person—as well as no nation—can truly exist half slave and half free that he has embroidered upon his banners the significant word NOW. The Negro is saying that the time has come for our nation to take that firm stride into freedom—not simply toward freedom—which will pay a long-overdue debt to its citizens of color.

For years now I have heard the word "Wait!" It rings in the ear of every Negro with piercing familiarity. This "Wait" has almost always meant "Never." We must come to see, with one of our distinguished jurists, that "justice too long delayed is justice denied."

··G··

GANDHI

Gandhi was probably the first person in history to lift the love ethic of Jesus above mere interaction between individuals to a powerful and effective social force on a large scale. Love for Gandhi was a potent instrument for social and collective transformation.

GHETTOS

As long as we go on building Negro central cities ringed by white suburbs we are inviting disaster.

GOAL

I refuse to accept the idea that the "isness" of man's present nature makes him morally incapable of reaching up for the eternal "oughtness" that forever confronts him.

GOD

I am convinced that the universe is under the control of a loving purpose, and that in the struggle for righteousness man has cosmic companionship. Behind the harsh appearances of the world there is a benign power. To say that this God is personal is not to make him a finite object besides other objects or attribute to him the limitations of human personality; it is to take what is finest and noblest in our consciousness and affirm its perfect existence in him.

We must never feel that God will, through some breathtaking miracle or a wave of the hand, cast evil out of the world. As long as we believe this we will pray unanswerable prayers and ask God to do things that he will never do.

This would be an unbearable world were God to have only

a single light, but we may be consoled that God has two lights: a light to guide us in the brightness of the day when hopes are fulfilled and circumstances are favorable, and a light to guide us in the darkness of the midnight when we are thwarted and the slumbering giants of gloom and hopelessness rise in our souls.

I am convinced of the reality of a personal God. . . . In the past the idea of a personal God was little more than a metaphysical category that I found theologically and philosophically satisfying. Now it is a living reality that has been validated in the experiences of everyday life. God has been profoundly real to me in recent years.

GOD AND EVIL

A healthy religion rises above the idea that God wills evil. Although God permits evil in order to preserve the freedom of man, He does not cause evil.

GOD AND MAN

The real weakness of the idea that God will do everything is its false conception of both God and man. It makes God so absolutely sovereign that man is absolutely helpless. It makes man so absolutely depraved that he can do nothing but wait on God. It sees the world as so contaminated with sin that God totally transcends it and touches it only here and there through a mighty invasion. This view ends up with a God who is a despot and not a Father. It ends up with a pessimism concerning human nature that leaves man little more than a helpless worm crawling through the morass of an evil world.

Racial justice, a genuine possibility in our nation and in the world, will come neither by our frail and often misguided efforts nor by God imposing his will on wayward men, but when enough people open their lives to God and allow him to pour his triumphant, divine energy into their souls. Our age-old and noble dream of a world of peace may yet become a reality, but it will come neither by man working alone nor by God destroying the wicked schemes of men, but when men so open their lives to God that he may fill them with love, mutual respect, understanding, and good will. Social salvation will come only through man's willing acceptance of Gods' mighty gift.

The idea that man expects God to do everything leads inevitably to a callous misuse of prayer. For if God does everything, man then asks him for anything, and God becomes little more than a "cosmic bellhop" who is summoned for every trivial need. Or God is considered so omnipotent and man so powerless that prayer is a substitute for work and intelligence.

GOOD AND EVIL

The history of man is the story of the struggle between good and evil.

Noncooperation with evil is just as much a moral duty as is cooperation with good.

Evil may so shape events that Caesar will occupy a palace and Christ a cross, but one day that same Christ will rise up and split history into A.D. and B.C., so that even the life of Caesar must be dated by his name.

GOOD WILL

Unenforceable obligations are beyond the reach of the laws of society. They concern inner attitudes, genuine person-to-person relations, and expressions of compassion which law books cannot regulate and jails cannot rectify. Such obligations are met by one's commitment to an inner law, written on the heart.

The ultimate solution to the race problem lies in the willingness of men to obey the unenforceable.

GRACE AND JUSTICE

God has two outstretched arms. One is strong enough to surround us with justice, and one is gentle enough to embrace us with grace.

GRADUALISM

It was ridiculous to speak of timing when the clock of history showed that the Negro had already suffered one hundred years of delay.

Some of the most vocal liberals believe they have a valid basis for demanding that, in order to gain certain rights, the Negro ought to pay for them out of the funds of patience and passivity which he has stored up for so many years. What these people do not realize is that gradualism and moderation are not the answer to the great moral indictment which, in the Revolution of 1963, finally came to stand in the center of our national stage.

GREATNESS

Very seldom are we able to affirm greatness in an unqualified sense. Following almost every affirmation of greatness is the conjunction "but."

GROUP MORALITY

We have not made a single gain in civil rights without determined legal and nonviolent pressure. Lamentably it is an historical fact that privileged groups seldom give up their privileges voluntarily. Individuals may see the moral light and voluntarily give up their unjust posture; but, as Reinhold Niebuhr has reminded us, groups tend to be more immoral than individuals.

··H··

HATE

Let no man pull you so low as to hate him.

Hate is a contagion; . . . it grows and spreads as a disease; . . . No society is so healthy that it can automatically maintain its immunity.

We were all involved in the death of John Kennedy. We tolerated hate; we tolerated the sick stimulation of violence in all walks of life; and we tolerated the differential application of law, which said that a man's life was sacred only if we agreed with his views. This may explain the cascading grief that flooded the country in late November. We mourned a man who had become the pride of the nation, but we grieved as well for ourselves because we knew we were sick.

We never get rid of an enemy by meeting hate with hate; we get rid of an enemy by getting rid of enmity.

Returning hate for hate multiplies hate, adding deeper darkness to a night already devoid of stars. Darkness cannot drive out darkness; only light can do that. Hate cannot drive out hate; only love can do that. Hate multiplies hate, violence multiplies violence, and toughness multiplies toughness in a descending spiral of destruction.

We must realize so many people are taught to hate us that they are not totally responsible for their hate.

To meet hate with retaliatory hate would do nothing but intensify the existence of evil in the universe. . . . We must meet the forces of hate with the power of love; we must meet physical force with soul force. Our aim must never be to defeat or humiliate the white man, but to win his friendship and understanding.

Upheaval after upheaval has reminded us that modern man is traveling along a road called hate, in a journey that will bring us to destruction and damnation.

Our civil rights efforts have not aroused hatred. They have revealed hatred that already existed. There is no doubt about the fact that there are many latent hostilities existing within certain white groups in the North, and what has happened now is that these latent hostilities have come out in the open.

HATE AND FEAR

Hate is rooted in fear, and the only cure for fear-hate is love.

HEAD AND HEART

Unlike physical blindness that is usually inflicted upon individuals as a result of natural forces beyond their control, intellectual and moral blindness is a dilemma which man inflicts upon himself by his tragic misuse of freedom and his failure to use his mind to its fullest capacity. One day we will learn that the heart can never be totally right if the head is totally wrong. This is not to say that the head can be right if the heart is wrong. Only through the bringing together of head and heart—intelligence and goodness—shall man rise to a fulfillment of his true nature.

HEROES

For every noted hero, there have been hundreds who have labored humbly and anonymously in the vineyard of freedom.

HEROISM

. . . **Negro.** One day the South will recognize its real heroes. They will be the James Merediths, with the noble sense of purpose that enables them to face jeering and hostile mobs, and with the agonizing loneliness that characterizes the life of the pioneer. They will be old, oppressed, battered Negro women, symbolized in a seventy-two-year-old woman in Montgomery, Alabama, who rose up with a sense of dignity and with her people decided not to ride segregated buses, and who responded with ungrammatical profundity to one who inquired about her weariness: "My feets is tired, but my soul is at rest." . . . One day the South will know that when these disinherited children of God sat down at lunch counters, they were in reality standing up for what is best in the American dream and for the most sacred values in our Judaeo-Christian heritage, thereby bringing our nation back to those great wells of democracy which were dug deep by the founding fathers in their formulation of the Constitution and the Declaration of Independence.

HISTORY

History is ultimately guided by spirit, not matter.

History does not pose problems without eventually producing solutions.

To become the instruments of a great idea is a privilege that history gives only occasionally.

. . . **Continuity.** Whether we realize it or not, each of us is eternally "in the red." We are everlasting debtors to known and unknown men and women.

HOPE

We must accept finite disappointment, but we must never lose infinite hope.

In the inevitable moments when all seems hopeless, men know that without hope they cannot really live, and in agonizing desperation they cry for the bread of hope.

HUMANISM

Believing neither in God nor in the existence of any supernatural power, the humanist affirms that man is the highest form of being which has evolved in the natural universe.

Give people a fair chance and a decent education, and they

will save themselves. This idea, sweeping across the modern world like a plague, has ushered God out and escorted man in and has substituted human ingenuity for divine guidance.

HUMAN NATURE

Man by his own power can never cast evil from the world. The humanist's hope is an illusion, based on too great an optimism concerning the inherent goodness of human nature.

Negroes are human, not superhuman. Like all people, they have differing personalities, diverse financial interests and varied aspirations. There are Negroes who will never fight for freedom. There are Negroes who will seek profit for themselves alone from the struggle. There are even some Negroes who will cooperate with their oppressors. These facts should distress no one. Every minority and every people has its share of opportunists, profiteers, freeloaders and escapists. The hammer blows of discrimination, poverty and segregation must warp and corrupt some. No one can pretend that because a people may be oppressed, every individual member is virtuous and worthy. The real issue is whether in the great mass the dominant characteristics are decency, honor and courage.

. . . **Goodness.** The nonviolent resister never lets this idea go, that there is something within human nature that can respond to goodness. So that a Jesus of Nazareth or a Mohandas Gandhi, can appeal to human beings and appeal to that element of goodness within them, and a Hitler can appeal to the element of evil within them. . . . And so the individuals who believe . . . in nonviolence and our struggle in the South somehow believe . . . that there is something within human nature that can be changed, and this stands at the top of the whole philosophy of the student movement (against segregation) and the philosophy of nonviolence.

HYPOCRISY

Millions of Peace Corps dollars are being invested in Africa because of the votes of some men who fight unrelentingly to prevent African ambassadors from holding membership in their diplomatic clubs or establish residency in their particular neighborhoods.

Millions of missionary dollars have gone to Africa from the hands of church people who would die a million deaths before they would permit a single African the privilege of worshiping in their congregation.

·· I ··

IGNORANCE

Sincerity and conscientiousness in themselves are not enough. History has proven that these noble virtues may degenerate into tragic vices. Nothing in all the world is more dangerous than sincere ignorance and conscientious stupidity.

. . . **Danger.** There are those who sincerely feel that disarmament is an evil and international negotiation is an abominable waste of time. Our world is threatened by the grim prospect of atomic annihilation because there are still too many men who know not what they do.

IMPARTIALITY

In all too many Northern communities a sort of quasi-liberalism prevails, so bent on seeing all sides that it fails to become dedicated to any side. It is so objectively analytical that it is not subjectively committed.

IMPERSONALNESS

Living in a world which has become oppressively impersonal, many of us have come to feel that we are little more than numbers. Ralph Borsodi in an arresting picture of a world wherein numbers have replaced persons writes that the modern mother is often maternity case No. 8434, and her child, after being fingerprinted and footprinted, becomes No. 8003, and that a funeral in a large city is an event in Parlor B with Class B flowers and decorations at which Preacher No. 14 officiates and Musician No. 84 sings Selection No. 174. Bewildered by this tendency to reduce man to a card in a vast index, man desperately searches for the bread of love.

The hardhearted individual never sees people as people, but

rather as mere objects or as impersonal cogs in an ever-turning wheel. In the vast wheel of industry, he sees men as hands. In the massive wheel of big city life, he sees men as digits in a multitude. In the deadly wheel of army life, he sees men as numbers in a regiment. He depersonalizes life.

INDECISIVENESS

Neither sympathy nor patience should be used as excuses for indecisiveness. They must be guiding principles for all of our actions, rather than substitutes for action itself.

INFLUENCE

Most people, and Christians in particular, are thermometers that record or register the temperature of majority opinion, not thermostats that transform and regulate the temperature of society.

IMPROVEMENT

The prohibition of barbaric behavior, while beneficial to the victim, does not constitute the attainment of equality or freedom. A man may cease beating his wife without thereby creating a wholesome marital relationship.

INTEGRATION

The Negro himself has a decisive role to play if integration is to become a reality. Indeed, if first-class citizenship is to become a reality for the Negro he must assume the primary responsibility for making it so. Integration is not some lavish dish that the federal government or the white liberal will pass out on a silver platter while the Negro merely furnishes the appetite. One of the damaging effects of past segregation on the personality of the Negro may well be that he has been victimized with the delusion that others should be more concerned than himself about his citizenship rights.

The Negro's aim is to bring about complete integration in American life.

Harmonizing of peoples of vastly different cultural levels is complicated and frequently abrasive.

This is no day to pay lip service to integration, we must pay *life* service to it.

We (Negroes) must be able to face up honestly to our own shortcomings. We must act in such a way as to make possible a coming together of white people and colored people on the basis of a real harmony of interests and understanding. We seek an integration based on mutual respect.

There are those who contend that integration can come only through education, for no other reason than that morals cannot be legislated. I choose, however, to be dialectical at this point. It isn't whether education or legislation; it is both legislation and education.

To paraphrase Biblical history, they (the colored peoples of the world) have broken loose from the Egypt of colonialism and imperialism, and they are now moving through the wilderness of adjustment toward the promised land of cultural integration.

. . . **Commitment.** There is a pressing need for a liberalism in the North which is truly liberal, a liberalism that firmly believes in integration in its own community as well as in the Deep South. It is one thing to agree that the goal of integration is morally and legally right; it is another thing to commit oneself positively and actively to the ideal of integration—the former is intellectual assent, the latter is actual belief.

. . . **Fear.** There is not only the job of freeing the Negro from the bondage of segration but also the responsibility of freeing his white brothers from the bondage of fears concerning integration.

. . . **Housing.** We have seen in the effort to integrate schools, even in the more tolerant northern urban centers, that many reasonably unbigoted persons assume a new posture with the introduction of unfamiliar problems into school systems where they have a personal interest. In the quest for genuinely integrated housing, the intensity of opposition from many who considered themselves free of prejudice made it clear that this struggle will be attained by tenacious difficulties.

In the North and all over the country people will adjust to living next door to a Negro, once they know that it has to be done, once realtors stop all of the block busting, the panic peddling and all of that. When the law makes it clear, and it is vigorously enforced, we will see that people will not only adjust, but they will finally come to the point that even their attitudes are changed.

. . . **Love.** Neither repression, massive resistance, nor aggressive violence will cast out the fear of integration; only love and goodwill can do that.

. . . **Procrastination.** We can, of course, try to temporize, negotiate small, inadequate changes and prolong the timetable of freedom in the hope that the narcotics of delay will dull the pain of progress. We can try, but we shall certainly fail. The shape of the world will not permit us the luxury of gradualism and procrastination.

INTELLIGENCE

As the chief moral guardian of the community, the church must implore men to be good and well-intentioned and must extol the virtues of kindheartedness and conscientiousness. But somewhere along the way the church must remind men that devoid of intelligence, goodness and conscientiousness will become brutal forces leading to shameful crucifixions. Never must the church tire of reminding men that they have a moral responsibility to be intelligent.

A nation or a civilization that continues to produce softminded men purchases its own spiritual death on an installment plan.

Throughout the New Testament we are reminded of the need for enlightenment. We are commanded to love God, not only with our hearts and souls, but also with our minds. When the Apostle Paul noticed the blindness of many of his opponents, he said, "I bear them record that they have a zeal for God, but not according to knowledge." Over and again the Bible reminds us of the danger of zeal without knowledge and sincerity without intelligence.

INTERDEPENDENCE

In the final analysis, all men are interdependent and are thereby involved in a single process. We are inevitably our brother's keeper because of the interrelated structure of reality. No nation or individual can live in isolation.

"I" cannot reach fulfillment without "thou." The self cannot be self without other selves.

We do not finish breakfast without being dependent on more than half of the world. When we arise in the morning, we go into the bathroom where we reach for a sponge which is provided for us by a Pacific Islander. We reach for soap that is created for us by a Frenchman. The towel is provided by a Turk. Then at the table we drink coffee which is provided for us by a South American, or tea by a Chinese, or cocoa by a West African. Before we leave for our jobs we are beholden to more than half the world.

INTERMARRIAGE

The continual outcry concerning intermarriage is a distortion of the real issue. . . . The Negro's primary aim is to be the white man's brother, not his brother-in-law.

INTERRELATEDNESS

As long as there is poverty in the world I can never be rich, even if I have a billion dollars. As long as diseases are rampant and millions of people in the world cannot expect to live more than twenty-eight or thirty years, I can never be totally healthy even if I just got a good check-up at Mayo Clinic. I can never be what I ought to be until you are what you ought to be. This is the way our world is made.

INTIMIDATION

Selma (Alabama) involves more than disenfranchisement.

Its inner texture reveals overt and covert forms of terror and intimidation—that uniquely Southern form of existence for Negroes in which life is a constant state of acute defensiveness and deprivation.

Sheriff P. C. Jenkins has held office in Wilcox (County, Alabama) for twenty-six years. He is a local legend because when he wants a Negro for a crime, he merely sends out word and the Negro comes in to be arrested. This is intimidation and degradation reminiscent only of chattel slavery.

· · J · ·

JESUS

Society must have its standards, norms, and mores. It must have its legal checks and judicial restraints. Those who fall below the standards and those who disobey the laws are often left in a dark abyss of condemnation and have no hope for a second chance. . . . Jesus eloquently affirmed from the cross a higher law. He knew that the old eye-for-an-eye philosophy would leave everyone blind. He did not seek to overcome evil with evil. He overcame evil with good. Although crucified by hate, he responded with aggressive love.

JUSTICE

Even today there still exists in the South—and in certain areas of the North—the license that our society allows to unjust officials who implement their authority in the name of justice to practice injustice against minorities. Where, in the days of slavery, social license and custom placed the unbridled power of the whip in the hands of overseers and masters, today—especially in the southern half of the nation—armies of officials are clothed in uniform, invested with authority, armed with the instruments of violence and death and conditioned to believe that they can intimidate, maim or kill Negroes with the same recklessness that once motivated the slaveowner. If one doubts this conclusion, let him search the records and find how rarely in any southern state a police officer has been punished for abusing a Negro.

Society must protect the robbed and punish the robber.

When the cry for justice has hardened into a palpable force, it becomes irresistible. This is a truth which wise leadership and a sensible society ultimately come to realize.

We have a strong feeling that in our struggle we have cosmic companionship. This is why our movement is often referred to as a spiritual movement. We feel that the universe is on the side of right. There is something in this universe which justifies Carlyle in saying: "No lie can live forever." There is something in this universe which justifies William Cullen Bryant in saying: "Truth crushed to earth will rise again."

Even though the arc of the moral universe is long, it bends toward justice.

JUSTICE AND INJUSTICE

The nonviolent resister has the vision to see that the basic tension is not between races. As I like to say to the people in Montgomery: "The tension in this city is not between white people and Negro people. The tension is, at bottom, between justice and injustice, between the forces of light and the forces of darkness. And if there is a victory, it will be a victory not merely for fifty thousand Negroes, but a victory for justice and the forces of light. We are out to defeat injustice and not white persons who may be unjust."

· · K · ·

KU KLUX KLAN

Determined to preserve segregation at any cost, . . . (the Ku Klux Klan) employs methods that are crude and primitive. It draws its members from underprivileged groups who see in the Negro's rising status a political and economic threat. Although the Klan is impotent politically and openly denounced from all sides, it remains a dangerous force which thrives on racial and religious bigotry. Because of its past history, whenever the Klan moves there is fear of violence.

$\cdot\cdot L \cdot\cdot$

LABOR

Labor leaders must continue to recognize that labor has a great stake in the struggle for civil rights, if only because the forces that are anti-Negro are usually anti-labor too.

. . . **Leadership.** Organized labor, not only on the national level but frequently on the local level as well, is lacking today in statesmanship, vigor and modernity.

. . . **Unions.** Labor unions can play a tremendous role in making economic justice a reality for the Negro. Trade unions are engaged in a struggle to advance the economic welfare of those American citizens whose wages are their livelihood. Since the American Negro is virtually nonexistent as the owner and manager of mass production industry, he must depend on the payment of wages for his economic survival.

The Negro has the right to expect the resources of the American trade union movement to be used in assuring him— like all the rest of its members—of a proper place in American society. He has gained this right along with all the other workers whose mutual efforts have built this country's free and democratic trade unions.

White and Negro workers have mutual aspirations for a fairer share of the products of industries and farms. Both seek job security, old-age security, health and welfare protection. The organized labor movement, which has contributed so much to the economic security and well-being of millions, must concentrate its powerful forces on bringing economic emancipation to white and Negro by organizing them together in social equality.

LAW

The law itself is a form of education. The words of the Supreme Court, of Congress, and of the Constitution are eloquent instructors.

There is a strain that runs through all (lawyers), be they Negro or white, conservative or radical, rich or poor. It is an immutable commitment to the philosophy that, with all of its uncertainties and weaknesses, the law is majestic and the judicial process supreme.

The law does not seek to change one's internal feelings; it seeks rather to control the external effects of those internal feelings. For instance, the law cannot make a man love me—religion and education must do that—but it can control his desire to lynch me.

. . . **Equal Protection.** Equal protection of the law is still substantially a national myth and a national disgrace in the reality of Negro life.

. . . **Implementation.** When . . . legislation becomes law, its vitality and power will depend as much on its implementation as on the strength of its declaration.

. . . **Ineffectiveness.** To launch a program with high-minded goals and to fail to safeguard it from opportunists and enemies amounts to sabotage, whether deliberate or undeliberate.

. . . **Just and Unjust.** An unjust law is a code that a numerical or power majority group compels a minority group to obey but does not make binding on itself. This is *difference* made legal. By the same token, a just law is a code that a majority compels a minority to follow and that it is willing to follow itself. This is *sameness* made legal.

There are two types of laws: just and unjust. I would be the first to advocate obeying just laws. One has not only a legal but a moral responsibility to obey just laws. Conversely, one has a moral responsibility to disobey unjust laws. I would agree with St. Augustine that "an unjust law is no law at all."

A just law is a law that squares with a moral law. It is a law that squares with that which is right, so that any law that uplifts human personality is a just law. Whereas that law which is out of harmony with the moral is a law which does not square with the moral law of the universe. It does not square with the law of God, so for that reason it is unjust and any law that degrades the human personality is an unjust law.

. . . **Legal Services.** Legal services accorded to our nonviolent armies of today are like plasma to the wounded in military combat.

. . . **Unenforced.** The ordinary Negro . . . knows how many laws exist in northern states and cities that prohibit discrimination in housing, in education and in employment; he knows how many overlapping commissions exist to enforce the terms of these laws—and he knows how he lives. The ubiquitous discrimination in his daily life tells him that more laws on paper no matter how breath-taking their terminology, will not guarantee that he will live in a "masterpiece of civilization."

LAW ENFORCEMENT

In the South we have had the hatred, the violence, the vitriolic and vituperative words of the mobs on the one hand, but often these mobs have been aided and abetted by the law and by law enforcement agents. I think the difference is (in northern cities) that we have the violence of the mobs, but at least the law enforcement agents are trying to preserve a degree of law and order.

LAWLESSNESS

There is a dangerous silence today which unintentionally encourages evil to flourish. Today lawlessness stalks in altogether too many sections of the Southland. The majesty of the law becomes more and more tarnished each day as scores of Negro churches are burned and bombed, as millions of Negroes are blatantly disenfranchised, as our homes are dynamited, and as innocent individuals are wantonly murdered.

So long as heinous crimes go unpunished, there develops a scorn and contempt for the legal process which bodes danger to our democracy.

LAWYERS

The road to freedom is now a highway because lawyers throughout the land, yesterday and today, have helped clear the obstructions, have helped eliminate roadblocks, by their selfless, courageous espousal of difficult and unpopular causes.

If the legal profession would share the passion and action of our time, it has the strength to achieve magnificent goals.

LEADERSHIP

The urgency of the hour calls for leaders of wise judgment and sound integrity—leaders not in love with money but in love with justice; leaders not in love with publicity, but in love with humanity; leaders who can subject their particular egos to the greatness of the cause.

The honors and privileges . . . that often come as a result of leadership constitute only one side of the picture. The greater the privileges, the greater the responsibilities and sacrifices.

There comes a time in the atmosphere of leadership when a man surrounded by loyal friends and allies realizes he has come face to face with himself.

The New Testament admonishes us that the people cannot hear if the trumpet makes an uncertain sound. What is their hope if the trumpet makes no sound at all?

LEGISLATION

Morals cannot be legislated, but behavior can be regulated. The law cannot make an employer love me, but it can keep him from refusing to hire me because of the color of my skin.

You can't make a man, through legal strictures and judicial decrees of executive orders, love somebody else. But we aren't trying to legislate love. We are trying to legislate issues that regulate behavior. Even though morality cannot be legislated, behavior can be regulated. While the law cannot change the heart, it can certainly restrain the heartless.

. . . **Desegregation.** It may be true that you can't legislate integration, but you can certainly legislate desegregation.

LIBERALISM

Liberalism provided me with an intellectual satisfaction that I had never found in fundamentalism. I became so enamored of the insights of liberalism that I almost fell into the trap of accepting uncritically everything it encompassed.

There are aspects of liberalism that I hope to cherish always: its devotion to the search for truth, its insistence on an open and analytical mind, and its refusal to abandon the best lights of reason. The contribution of liberalism to the philological-historical criticism of biblical literature has been of immeasurable value and should be defended with religious and scientific passion.

LIBERALISM AND NEO-ORTHODOXY

Although I rejected some aspects of liberalism, I never came to an all-out acceptance of neo-orthodoxy. While I saw neo-orthodoxy as a helpful corrective for a sentimental liberalism, I felt that it did not provide an adequate answer to basic questions. If liberalism was too optimistic concerning human nature, neo-orthodoxy was too pessimistic.

LIFE

The length of life as we shall think of it here is not its duration or its longevity, but it is the push of a life forward to achieve its personal ends and ambitions. It is the inward concern for one's own welfare. The breadth of life is the outward concern for the welfare of others. The height of life is the upward reach for God.

Life is something of a great triangle. At one angle stands the individual person, at the other angle stand other persons, and at the top stands the Supreme, Infinite Person, God. These three must meet in every individual life if that life is to be complete.

The end of life is not to be happy. The end of life is not to achieve pleasure and avoid pain. The end of life is to do the will of God, come what may.

Any complete life has the three dimensions . . . length, breadth, and height. The length of life is the inward drive to achieve one's personal ends and ambitions, an inward concern for one's own welfare and achievements. The breadth of life is the outward concern for the welfare of others. The height of life is the upward reach for God. Life at its best is a coherent triangle. At one angle is the individual person. At the other angle are other persons. At the tiptop is the Infinite Person, God. Without the due development of each part of the triangle, no life can be complete.

Like the rhythmic alternation in the natural order, life has the glittering sunlight of its summers and the piercing chill of its winters. Days of unutterable joy are followed by days of overwhelming sorrow. Life brings periods of flooding and periods of drought. . . . Christianity affirms that God . . . is able to give us the inner equilibrium to stand tall amid the trials and burdens of life. He is able to provide inner peace amid outer storms.

In a sense every day is judgment day, and we, through our deeds and words, our silence and speech, are constantly writing in the Book of Life.

. . . **Resources.** God does not forget his children who are the victims of evil forces. He gives us the interior resources to bear the burdens and tribulations of life.

LOVE

Love is the most durable power in the world.

When I say "love those who oppose you," I am not speaking of love in a sentimental or affectionate sense. It would be nonsense to urge men to love their oppressors in an affectionate sense. When I refer to love in this context I mean understanding good will.

Gandhi resisted evil with as much vigor and power as the violent resister, but he resisted with love instead of hate.

Since the white man's personality is greatly distorted by segregation, and his soul is greatly scarred, he needs the love of the Negro. The Negro must love the white man, because the white man needs his love to remove his tensions, insecurities, and fears.

We have before us the glorious opportunity to inject a new dimension of love into the veins of our civilization. . . . This love may well be the salvation of our civilization.

Love is the only force capable of transforming an enemy into a friend.

Every genuine expression of love grows out of a consistent and total surrender to God.

Everywhere and at all times, the love ethic of Jesus is a radiant light revealing the ugliness of our stale conformity.

There will be no permanent solution to the race problem until oppressed men develop the capacity to love their enemies. The darkness of racial injustice will be dispelled only by the light of forgiving love. For more than three centuries American Negroes have been battered by the iron rod of oppression, frustrated by day and bewildered by night by unbearable injustice, and burdened with the ugly weight of discrimination. Forced to live with these shameful conditions, we are tempted to become bitter and to retaliate with a corresponding hate. But if this happens, the new order we seek will be little more than a duplicate of the old order. We must in strength and humility meet hate with love.

I have discovered that the highest good is love. This principle is at the center of the cosmos. It is the great unifying force of life. God is love. He who loves has discovered the clue to the meaning of ultimate reality; he who hates stands in immediate candidacy for nonbeing.

There can be no deep disappointment where there is not deep love.

Toughmindedness without tenderheartedness is cold and detached, leaving one's life in a perpetual winter devoid of the warmth of spring and the gentle heat of summer.

We must evolve for all human conflict a method which rejects revenge, aggression and retaliation. The foundation of such a method is love.

The hardhearted person never truly loves. He engages in a crass utilitarianism which values other people mainly according to their usefulness to him. He never experiences the beauty of friendship, because he is too cold to feel affection for another and is too self-centered to share another's joy and sorrow. He is an isolated island. No outpouring of love links him with the mainland of humanity.

I refuse to accept the cynical notion that nation after nation must spiral down a militaristic stairway into the hell of thermonuclear destruction. I believe that unarmed truth and unconditional love will have the final word in reality.

Along with insistence on nonviolence goes the emphasis on love as the regulating ideal. In our struggle for justice, we have refused to succumb to the temptation of becoming bitter or indulging in a hate campaign.

We are not out to defeat or humiliate the white man, but to help him as well as ourselves. The festering sore of segregation debilitates the white man as well as the Negro. And so our struggle in Montgomery is not to win a victory over the white man. The real tension is not between white people and Negro people. The tension is at bottom between justice and injustice, between the forces of light and the forces of darkness. And if there is a victory it will be a victory not merely for 50,000 Negroes, but a victory for justice, freedom and democracy. This is at bottom the meaning of Christian love. It is understanding good will for all men. It seeks nothing in return. It is that love which loves the person who does the evil deed, while hating the deed which he does.

The law of love as an imperative is the norm for all of man's actions.

. . . **Charity.** You may give your goods to feed the poor, you may bestow great gifts to charity, and you may tower high in philanthropy, but if you have not love, your charity means nothing.

. . . **Nonviolence.** The whole Gandhian concept of *satyagraha* (*satya* is truth which equals love and *graha* is force; *satyagraha* thus means truth-force or love-force) was profoundly significant to me. . . . The Christian doctrine of love, operating through the Gandhian method of nonviolence, is one of the most potent weapons available to an oppressed people in their struggle for freedom.

. . . **of Enemies.** Far from being the pious injunction of a Utopian dreamer, the command to love one's enemy is an absolute necessity for our survival. Love even for enemies is the key to the solution of the problems of our world. Jesus is not an impractical idealist; he is the practical realist.

LOVE AND LIKE

It is pretty difficult to like some people. Like is sentimental, and it is pretty difficult to like someone bombing your home; it is pretty difficult to like somebody threatening your children; it is difficult to like congressmen who spend all of their time ·trying to defeat civil rights. But Jesus says love them, and love is greater than like. Love is understanding, redemptive, creative, good will for all men.

LUNCH-COUNTER SEGREGATION

There is a special humiliation for the Negro in having his money accepted at every department in a store except the lunch counter. Food is not only a necessity but a symbol, and our lunch-counter campaign had not only a practical but a symbolic importance.

· · M · ·

MAN

There is something within man which cannot be explained in chemical and biological terms, for man is more than a tiny vagary of whirling electrons.

Man cannot save himself, for man is not the measure of all things and humanity is not God. Bound by the chains of his own sin and finiteness, man needs a Saviour.

The ultimate measure of a man is not where he stands in moments of comfort and convenience, but where he stands at times of challenge and controversy.

. . . **Dualism.** Man is neither villain nor hero; he is rather both villain and hero.

Man has a dual citizenry. He lives both in time and in eternity; both in heaven and on earth.

. . . **Gentle and Tough.** Jesus reminds us that the good life combines the toughness of the serpent and the tenderness of the dove. To have serpentlike qualities devoid of dovelike qualities is to be passionless, mean, and selfish. To have dovelike without serpentlike qualities is to be sentimental, anemic, and aimless. We must combine strongly marked antitheses.

. . . **Good and Evil.** There is some good in the worst of us and some evil in the best of us.

. . . **Internal and External.** Each of us lives in two realms, the internal and the external. The internal is that realm of spiritual ends expressed in art, literature, morals, and religion. The instrumentalities are means by which we live. These include the house we live in, the car we drive, the clothes we wear, the economic resources we acquire—the material stuff we must have to exist. There is always a danger that we will permit the means by which we live to replace the ends for which we live, the internal to become lost in the external.

. . . **Physical Needs.** In any realistic doctrine of man we must be forever concerned about his physical and material well-being. When Jesus said that man cannot live by bread alone, he did not imply that men can live without bread. As Christians we must think not only about "mansions in the sky," but also about the slums and ghettos that cripple the human soul, not merely about streets in heaven "flowing with milk and honey," but also about the millions of people in this world who go to bed hungry at night.

. . . **Spiritual.** Man is a being of spirit. He moves up "the stairs of his concepts" into a wonder world of thought. Conscience speaks to him, and he is reminded of things divine. This is what the Psalmist meant when he said that man has been crowned with glory and honor.

(Man's) spiritual quality gives him the unique capacity to live on two levels. He is in nature, yet above nature; he is in space and time, yet above them. He can do creative things that lower animals could never do. Man can think a poem and write it; he can think a symphony and compose it; he can think of a great civilization and produce it. Because of this capacity, he is not bound completely by space and time.

MARXISM AND CAPITALISM

Nineteenth-century capitalism failed to see that life is social and Marxism failed and still fails to see that life is individual and personal. The Kingdom of God is neither the thesis of individual enterprise nor the antithesis of collective enterprise, but a synthesis which reconciles the truths of both.

MATERIALISM

Having no place for God or for eternal ideas, materialism is opposed to both theism and idealism.

Rich in goods and material resources, our standards of success are almost inextricably bound to the lust for acquisition.

The means by which we live are marvelous indeed. And yet something is missing. We have learned to fly the air like birds and swim the sea like fish, but we have not learned the simple art of living together as brothers.

Materialism is a weak flame that is blown out by the breath of mature thinking.

MATURITY

. . . **Self-Criticism.** One of the sure signs of maturity is the ability to rise to the point of self-criticism.

MEANS AND ENDS

In a real sense, the means represent the ideal in the making —the ends in process. So, in the long run, destructive means cannot bring about constructive ends because the ends are pre-existent in the means.

The Negro must work passionately and unrelentingly for full stature as a citizen, but he must not use inferior methods to gain it. He must never come to terms with falsehood, malice, hate, or destruction.

Over the last few years I have consistently preached that nonviolence demands that the means we use must be as pure as the ends we seek. So I have tried to make it clear that it is wrong to use immoral means to attain moral ends. But now I must affirm that it is just as wrong, or even more, to use moral means to preserve immoral ends.

MILITARY POWER

In a real sense, Waterloo symbolizes the doom of every Napoleon and is an eternal reminder to a generation drunk with military power that in the long run of history might does not make right and the power of the sword cannot conquer the power of the spirit.

. . . **Responsibility.** Every minister of the gospel has a mandate to stand up courageously for righteousness, to proclaim the eternal verities of the gospel, and to lead men from the darkness of falsehood and fear to the light of truth and love.

. . . **South.** Every white minister in the South must decide for himself which course he will follow. There is no single right strategy. The important thing is for every minister to dedicate himself to the Christian ideal of brotherhood, and be sure that he is doing something positive to implement it. He must never allow the theory that it is better to remain quiet and help the cause to become a rationalization for doing nothing.

MINORITY

Almost always the creative, dedicated minority has made the world better.

MISSIONS

. . . **Compassion.** Our missionary efforts fail when they are based on pity, rather than true compassion. Instead of seeking to do something *with* the African and Asian peoples, we have too often sought only to do something *for* them.

MISSISSIPPI

Mississippi is symbolic of every evil that American Negroes have long endured.

MOB PSYCHOLOGY

Man collectivized in the group, the tribe, the race, and the nation often sinks to levels of barbarity unthinkable even among lower animals.

MODERATES

I have almost reached the regrettable conclusion that the Negro's great stumbling block in his stride toward freedom is not the White Citizen's Councilor or the Ku Klux Klanner, but the white moderate, who is more devoted to "order" than to justice; who prefers a negative peace which is the absence of tension to a positive peace which is the presence of justice; who constantly says: "I agree with you in the goal you seek, but I cannot agree with your methods of direct action"; who paternalistically believes he can set the timetable for another man's freedom; who lives by a mythical concept of time and who constantly advises the Negro to wait for a "more convenient season."

MONEY

Money, like any other force such as electricity, is amoral and can be used for either good or evil.

MONTGOMERY

The skies did not fall when integrated buses finally traveled the streets of Montgomery.

The racial peace which had existed in Montgomery (before the bus boycott) was not a Christian peace. It was a pagan peace and it had been bought at too great a price.

MORALITY

Midnight is the hour when men desperately seek to obey the eleventh commandment, "Thou shalt not get caught." According to the ethic of midnight, the cardinal sin is to be caught and the cardinal virtue is to get by. It is all right to lie, but one must lie with real finesse. It is all right to steal, if one is so dignified that, if caught, the charge becomes embezzlement, not robbery. It is permissible even to hate, if one so dresses his hating in the garments of love that hating appears to be loving. The Darwinian concept of the survival of the fittest has been substituted by a philosophy of the survival of the slickest. This mentality has brought a tragic breakdown of moral standards, and the midnight of moral degeneration deepens.

Our hope for creative living lies in our ability to re-establish the spiritual ends of our lives in personal character and social justice. Without this spiritual and moral reawakening we shall destroy ourselves in the misuse of our own instruments.

MORAL LAW

There is a law in the moral world—a silent, invisible imperative, akin to the laws in the physical world—which reminds us that life will work only in a certain way. The Hitlers and the Mussolinis have their day, and for a period they may wield great power, spreading themselves like a green bay tree, but soon they are cut down like the grass and wither as the green herb.

The passing of systems that were born in injustice, nurtured in inequality, and reared in exploitation . . . represents the inevitable decay of any system based on principles that are not in harmony with the moral laws of the universe.

God . . . has placed within the very structure of this universe certain absolute moral laws. We can neither defy nor break them. If we disobey them, they will break us.

MUSIC

. . . **Courage.** I have stood in a meeting with hundreds of youngsters and joined in while they sang "Ain't Gonna Let Nobody Turn Me 'Round." It is not just a song; it is a resolve. A few minutes later, I have seen those same youngsters refuse to turn around from the onrush of a police dog, refuse to turn around before a pugnacious Bull Connor in command of men armed with power hoses. These songs bind us together, give us courage together, help us to march together.

MUTUALITY

All life is interrelated. All men are caught in an inescapable network of mutuality, tied in a single garment of destiny. Whatever affects one directly affects all indirectly. I can never be what I ought to be until you are what you ought to be, and you can never be what you ought to be until I am what I ought to be. This is the interrelated structure of reality.

Injustice anywhere is a threat to justice everywhere. . . . Whatever affects one directly, affects all indirectly. Never again can we afford to live with the narrow, provincial "outside agitator" idea. Anyone who lives inside the United States can never be considered an outsider anywhere within its bounds.

··N··

NATURE

At night we look up at the stars which bedeck the heavens like swinging lanterns of eternity. For the moment we may think we see all, but something reminds us that we do not see the law of gravitation that holds them there.

NEGROES

While still in the prison of segregation, we must ask, "How may we turn this liability into an asset?" By recognizing the necessity of suffering in a righteous cause, we may possibly achieve our humanity's full stature. To guard ourselves from bitterness, we need the vision to see in this generation's ordeals the opportunity to transfigure both ourselves and American society. Our present suffering and our nonviolent struggle to be free may well offer to Western civilization the kind of spiritual dynamic so desperately needed for survival.

The powerless morality of the Negro confronts the immorality of white power.

We are willing to make the Negro 100 per cent of a citizen in warfare, but reduce him to 50 per cent of a citizen on American soil. Half of all Negroes live in substandard housing and have half the income of whites. There is twice as much unemployment and infant mortality among Negroes. There were twice as many Negroes in combat in Vietnam at the beginning of 1967, and twice as many died in action—20.6 per cent—in proportion to their numbers in the population as whites.

The Negro, even in his bitterest moments, is not intent on killing white men to be free.

It would be a tragic indictment of both the self-respect and practical wisdom of the Negro if history reveals that at the height of the twentieth century the Negro spent more for frivolities than for the cause of freedom.

Every Negro, regardless of his educational or cultural level, carries the burden of centuries of deprivation and inferior status. The burden is with him every waking moment of his life—and often, through his dreams, dominates his sleeping moments as well. It diminishes his confidence and belittles his achievements. He is tormented by the overwhelming task of catching up.

The Negro had been an object of sympathy and wore the scars of deep grievances, but the nation had come to count on him as a creature who could quietly endure, silently suffer and patiently wait.

. . . **Americans.** Negroes expect their freedom, not as subjects of benevolence but as Americans who were at Bunker Hill, who toiled to clear the forests, drain the swamps, build the roads—who fought the wars and dreamed the dreams the founders of the nation considered to be an American birthright.

. . . **Apathy.** While there were always some (Negroes in Montgomery, Alabama) who struck out against segregation, the largest number (before the bus boycott) accepted it without apparent protest. Not only did they seem resigned to segregation per se; they also accepted the abuses and indignities which came with it. My predecessor at the Dexter Avenue Baptist Church—Rev. Vernon Johns—tells of an incident that illustrates the attitude of the people at this time. One day he boarded a bus and sat in one of the front seats reserved for whites only. The bus driver demanded that he move back. Mr. Johns refused. The operator then ordered him off the bus. Again Mr. Johns refused, until the driver agreed to return his fare. Before leaving, Mr. Johns stood in the aisle and asked how many of his people would follow him off the bus in protest. Not a single person responded.

. . . **Challenge.** In the new age many doors will be opening to us (Negroes) that were not open in the past, and the great challenge which we confront is to be prepared to enter these doors as they open.

. . . **Character.** The experience of Negro youth is as harsh and demanding as that of the pioneer on the untamed frontier. Because his struggle is complex, there is no place in it for the frivolous or rowdy. Knowledge and discipline are as indispensable as courage and self-sacrifice. Hence the forging of priceless qualities of character is taking place daily as a high moral goal is pursued.

. . . **Commitment.** The striking quality in Negro students I have met is the intensity and depth of their commitment. I am no longer surprised to meet attractive, stylishly-dressed young girls whose charm and personality would grace a junior prom and to hear them declare in unmistakably sincere terms, "Dr. King, I am ready to die if I must."

. . . **Economic Compensation.** Among the many vital jobs to be done, the nation must not only radically readjust its attitude toward the Negro in the compelling present, but must incorporate in its planning some compensatory consideration for the handicaps he has inherited from the past. It is impossible to create a formula for the future which does not take into account that our society has been doing something special *against* the Negro for hundreds of years. How then can he be absorbed into the mainstream of American life if we do not do something special *for* him now, in order to balance the equation and equip him to compete on a just and equal basis.

. . . **Low Wages.** Someone has been profiting from the low wages of Negroes. Depressed living standards for Negroes are a structural part of the economy. Certain industries are based upon the supply of low-wage, underskilled and immobile nonwhite labor. Hand-assembly factories, hospitals, service industries, housework, agriculture operations using itinerant labor, would all suffer shock, if not disaster, if the minimum wage were significantly raised. A hardening of opposition to the satisfaction of Negro needs must be anticipated as the (civil rights) movement presses against financial privilege.

. . . **Opportunity.** The future of the Negro college student has long been walled within the narrow walls of limited opportunity. Only a few professions could be practiced by Negroes and, but for a few exceptions, behind barriers of segregation in the North as well as the South. Few frustrations can compare with the experience of struggling with complex academic subjects, straining to absorb concepts which may never be used, or only half-utilized under conditions insulting to the trained mind.

. . . **Organization.** Negro leadership, long attuned to agitation, must now perfect the art of organization. The movement needs stable and responsible institutions in the communities to utilize the new strength of Negroes in altering social customs.

. . . **Political Apathy.** Political life, as a rule, did not attract the best elements of the Negro community, and white candidates who represented their views were few and far between. However, in avoiding the trap of domination by unworthy leaders, Negroes fell into the bog of political inactivity. They avoided victimization by any political group by withholding a significant commitment to any organization or individual.

. . . **Poverty Program.** Negroes must be brought into the very central structure of the whole poverty program.

. . . **Religion.** If we as a people have as much religion in our hearts as we have in our legs and feet, we could change the world.

. . . **Security.** A job in our industrial society is not necessarily equivalent to security. It is too often undercut by layoffs. No element of the working people suffers so acutely from layoffs as Negroes, traditionally the first fired and the last hired. They lack the seniority other workers accumulate because discrimination thwarts long-term employment. Negroes need the kind of employment that lasts the year through. They need the opportunities to advance on the jobs; they need the type of employment that feeds, clothes, educates and stabilizes the family.

The direction of Negro demands has to be toward some substantive security. This alone will revolutionize Negro life, including family relations and that part of the Negro psyche which has lately become conspicuous—the Negro male ego.

. . . **Self-Help.** From beyond the borders of his own land, the Negro had . . . watched the decolonization and liberation of nations in Africa and Asia since World War II. He knew that yellow, black and brown people had felt for years that the American Negro was too passive, unwilling to take strong measures to gain his freedom. He might have remembered the visit to this country of an African head of state, who was called upon by a delegation of prominent American Negroes. When they began reciting to him their long list of grievances, the visiting statesman had waved a weary hand and said: "I am aware of current events. I know everything you are telling me about what the white man is doing to the Negro. Now tell me: What is the Negro doing for himself?"

. . . **South.** The Negro's problem will not be solved by running away. He cannot listen to the glib suggestion of those who would urge him to migrate en masse to other sections of the country. By grasping his great opportunity in the South he can make a lasting contribution to the moral strength of the nation and set a sublime example of courage for generations yet unborn.

. . . **Standards.** America must seek its own ways of atoning for the injustices she has inflicted upon her Negro citizens. I do not suggest atonement for atonement's sake or because there is need for self-punishment. I suggest atonement as the moral and practical way to bring the Negro's standards up to a realistic level.

. . . **Students.** Not long ago the Negro collegian imitated the white collegian. In attire, in athletics, in social life, imitation was the rule. For the future, he looked to a professional life cast in the image of the middle class white professional. He imitated with such energy that Gunnar Myrdal described the ambitious Negro as "an exaggerated American." Today the imitation has ceased. The Negro collegian now initiates. Groping for unique forms of protest, he created the sit-ins and freedom rides. Overnight his white fellow students began to imitate him.

. . . **Unemployment.** There were two and one-half times as many jobless Negroes as whites in 1963, and their median income was half that of the white man.

Statistics that picture declining rates of unemployment veil the reality that Negro jobs are still substandard and evanescent. The instability of employment reflects itself in the fragile character of Negro ambitions and economic foundations.

In Harlem, almost 50 per cent of the employable youth, that is, the young people who ought to be working, are unemployed. . . . That presents dangerous social problems for the big cities of the North.

. . . **Unity.** Negro solidarity is a powerful growing force which no society may wisely ignore.

The weary and worn "outsider" charge, . . . we have faced in every community where we have gone to try to help. No Negro, in fact, no American, is an outsider when he goes to any community to aid the cause of freedom and justice. No Negro anywhere, regardless of his social standing, his financial status, his prestige and position, is an outsider so long as dignity and decency are denied to the humblest black child in Mississippi, Alabama or Georgia.

Our mutual sufferings had wrapped us all (Negroes) in a single garment of destiny. What happened to one happened to all.

Cambridge, Maryland, and Rome, Georgia, differed from one another in degrees of bitterness and brutality, but not in attitudes of resistance. From one perspective these engagements were all defeats for the movement. Yet from another viewpoint there were intangible elements of victory. Despite the worst these communities could inflict, they could not drive the Negroes apart. Their blows only served to unite our ranks, stiffen our resistance and tap our deepest resources of courage.

Every time one Negro school teacher is fired for believing in integration, a thousand others should be ready to take the same stand. If the oppressors bomb the home of one Negro for his protest, they must be made to realize that to press back the rising tide of the Negro's courage they will have to bomb hundreds more, and even then they will fail.

. . . **Voting.** By 1940 there were not more than 2,000 Negro voters in all Alabama. Today the number is closer to 50,000, but although this represents progress, it is still less than 10 per cent of all Negroes of voting age in the state. In 1954 there were some 30,000 Negroes of voting age in Montgomery County, but only a few more than 2,000 were registered.

. . . **World-Wide Struggle.** The liberation struggle in Africa has been the greatest single international influence on American Negro students. Frequently I hear them say that if their African brothers can break the bonds of colonialism surely the American Negro can break Jim Crow.

The Negro students are greatly concerned about their civil rights, and naturally the whole struggle in the world today has its implications in this country. I think this is really a part of the world-wide movement for freedom and human dignity. This isn't an isolated struggle, it's a part of the world-wide movement. And I'm sure that it will not automatically cease. It will cease only when the Negro people feel that they have achieved something.

The arresting upsurge of Africa and Asia is remote neither in time nor in space to the Negro of the South. Indeed, the determination of Negro Americans to win freedom from all forms of oppression springs from the same deep longing that motivates oppressed peoples all over the world.

NEGROES AND WHITES

Negroes acting alone and in a hostile posture toward all whites will do nothing more than demonstrate that their conditions of life are unendurable, and that they are unbearably angry. . . . A genuine Negro-white unity is the tactical foundation upon which past and future progress depends.

The section of the Civil Rights Act of 1964 which withholds federal aid when it is used discriminatorily in federally assisted programs has revolutionary implications. It ties the interests of whites who desperately need relief from their impoverishment to the Negro who has the same needs. The barriers of segregation are splintering under the strain of economic deprivation which cuts across caste lines.

To climb the economic ladder, Negro and white will have to steady it together, or both will fall.

NEGRO CITIZENSHIP

The Negro . . . is not seeking to dominate the nation, but simply wants the right to live as a first-class citizen, with all the responsibilities that good citizenship entails.

NEGRO EMANCIPATION

With the dawn of 1963, plans were afoot all over the land to celebrate the Emancipation Proclamation, the one-hundredth birthday of the Negro's liberation from bondage. . . . But alas! All the talk and publicity accompanying the centennial only served to remind the Negro that he still wasn't free, that he still lived a form of slavery disguised by certain niceties of complexity. As the then Vice-President, Lyndon B. Johnson, phrased it: "Emancipation was a Proclamation but not a fact." The pen of the Great Emancipator had moved the Negro into the sunlight of physical freedom, but actual conditions had left him behind in the shadow of political, psychological, social, economic and intellectual bondage.

NEGRO EQUALITY

Negroes are not innately inferior in academic, health, and moral standards. . . . When given equal opportunities, Negroes can demonstrate equal achievement.

NEGRO INFERIORITY

The Negro in Birmingham, like the Negro elsewhere in this

nation, had been skillfully brainwashed to the point where he had accepted the white man's theory that he, as a Negro, was inferior. He wanted to believe that he was the equal of any man; but he didn't know where to begin or how to resist the influences that had conditioned him to take the least line of resistance and go along with the white man's views.

NEGRO MOVEMENT

We must work on two fronts. On the one hand, we must continue to resist the system of segregation which is the basic cause of our lagging standards; on the other hand we must work constructively to improve the standards themselves. There must be a rhythmic alternation between attacking the causes and healing the effects.

. . . **Press Coverage.** Normally Negro activities are the object of attention in the press only when they are likely to lead to some dramatic outbreak, or possess some bizarre quality. The March (on Washington) was the first organized Negro operation which was accorded respect and coverage commensurate with its importance. The millions who viewed it on television were seeing an event historic not only because of the subject, but because it was being brought into their homes.

NEGRO RESPONSIBILITY

We must not let the fact that we are the victims of injustice lull us into abrogating responsibility for our own lives.

In this period of social change, the Negro must come to see that there is much he himself can do about his plight. He may be uneducated or poverty-stricken, but these handicaps must not prevent him from seeing that he has within his being the power to alter his fate.

NEGRO REVOLUTION

The Revolution is not indicative of a sudden loss of patience within the Negro. The Negro had never really been patient in the pure sense of the word. The posture of silent waiting was forced upon him psychologically because he was shackled physically.

Just as lightning makes no sound until it strikes, the Negro Revolution generated quietly. But when it struck, the revealing flash of its power and the impact of its sincerity and fervor displayed a force of frightening intensity. Three hundred years of humiliation, abuse and deprivation cannot be expected to find voice in a whisper.

NEGRO UPRISING

. . . **Summer 1963.** Seen in perspective, the summer of 1963 was historic partly because it witnessed the first offensive in history launched by Negroes along a broad front. The heroic but spasmodic and isolated slave revolts of the ante-bellum South had fused, more than a century later, into a simultaneous, massive assault against segregation. And the virtues so long regarded as the exclusive property of the white South—gallantry, loyalty and pride—had passed to the Negro demonstrators in the heat of the summer's battles.

Witnessing the drama of Negro progress elsewhere in the world, witnessing a level of conspicuous consumption at home exceeding anything in our history, it was natural that by 1963 Negroes would rise with resolution and demand a share of governing power, and living conditions measured by American standards rather than by the standards of colonial impoverishment.

In 1963 the Negro, who had realized for many years that he was not truly free, awoke from a stupor of inaction with the cold dash of realization that 1963 meant one hundred years after Lincoln gave his autograph to the cause of his freedom.

The striking thing about the nonviolent crusade of 1963 was that so few felt the sting of bullets or the clubbing of billies and nightsticks. Looking back, it becomes obvious that the oppressors were restrained not only because the world was looking but also because, standing before them, were hundreds, sometimes thousands, of Negroes who for the first time dared to look back at a white man, eye to eye.

NEGRO VOTING

Even where the polls are open to all, Negroes have shown themselves too slow to exercise their voting privileges. . . . In the past, apathy was a moral failure. Today, it is a form of moral and political suicide.

One of the most significant steps the Negro can take is the short walk to the voting booth.

When the full power of the ballot is available to my people it will not be exercised merely to advance our cause alone. We have learned in the course of our freedom struggle that the needs of twenty million Negroes are not truly separable from those of the nearly 200 million whites and Negroes in America, all of whom will benefit from a colorblind land of plenty that provides for the nourishment of each man's body, mind and spirit.

NEW NEGRO

The tension which we are witnessing in race relations today can be explained, in part, by the revolutionary change in the Negro's evaluation of himself, and determination to struggle and sacrifice until the walls of segregation have finally been crushed by the battering rams of surging justice.

The new Negro has acquired a new self-respect and a new sense of dignity. He lacks the fear which once characterized his behavior. He once used duplicity—a survival technique— but now he has developed an honesty.

One can never understand the bus protest in Montgomery without understanding that there is a new Negro in the South, with a new sense of dignity and destiny.

(Segregationists in Montgomery, Alabama) thought they were dealing with a group who could be cajoled or forced to do whatever the white man wanted them to do. They were not aware that they were dealing with Negroes who had been freed from fear. And so every move they made proved to be a mistake. It could not be otherwise, because their methods were geared to the "old Negro," and they were dealing with a "new Negro."

Once plagued with a tragic sense of inferiority resulting from the crippling effects of slavery and segregation, the Negro has now been driven to reevaluate himself. He has come to feel that he is somebody. His religion reveals to him that God loves all His children and that the important thing about man is not "his specificity but his fundamentum"—not the texture of his hair or the color of his skin but his eternal worth to God.

The Revolution of the Negro not only attacked the external cause of his misery, but revealed him to himself. He was *somebody*. He had a sense of *somebodiness*. He was *impatient* to be free.

Negroes have discovered the fighting spirit, and the power, each within himself. Voluntarily facing death in many places, they have relied upon their own united ranks for strength and protection. . . . Helplessness was replaced by confidence as hundreds of thousands of Negroes discovered that organization, together with nonviolent direct action, was explosively, powerfully and socially transforming.

Negroes are not now merely a subject of change but an active organ of change. This is the new political equation in contemporary society.

NONCOMMITMENT

Shallow understanding from people of good will is more frustrating than absolute misunderstanding from people of ill will. Lukewarm acceptance is much more bewildering than outright rejection.

NONCONFORMISTS

The hope of a secure and livable world lies with disciplined nonconformists, who are dedicated to justice, peace, and brotherhood. The trailblazers in human, academic, scientific, and religious freedom have always been nonconformists. In any cause that concerns the progress of mankind, put your faith in the nonconformists!

NONCONFORMITY

Human salvation lies in the hands of the creatively maladjusted.

Nonconformity in itself . . . may not necessarily be good and may at times possess neither transforming nor redemptive power. Nonconformity per se contains no saving value, and may represent in some circumstances little more than a form of exhibitionism.

NONVIOLENCE

Nonviolence means avoiding not only external physical violence but also internal violence of spirit. You not only refuse to shoot a man, but you refuse to hate him.

The nonviolent resister must often express his protest through noncooperation or boycotts, but he realizes that these are not ends themselves; they are merely means to awaken a sense of moral shame in the opponent. The end is redemption and reconciliation. The aftermath of nonviolence is the creation of the beloved community, while the aftermath of violence is tragic bitterness.

There is a great distinction between individuals who are nonviolently engaged in pursuit of basic constitutional rights and who in the process face violence and face hatred perpetrated against them, and individuals who aggressively throw Molotov cocktails and engage in riots.

Nonviolent direct action did not originate in America, but it found its natural home in this land, where refusal to cooperate with injustice was an ancient and honorable tradition and where Christian forgiveness was written into the minds and hearts of good men.

Whatever measure of influence I may now have as a result of the importance which the world attaches to the Nobel Peace Prize, I must use that influence to bring the philosophy of nonviolence to all the world's people who grapple with the age-old problem of racial injustice. I must, somehow, convince them of the effectiveness of this weapon which cuts without wounding; this weapon which ennobles the man who wields it.

The nonviolent approach does something to the hearts and souls of those committed to it. It gives them new self-respect. It calls up resources of strength and courage that they did not know they had. Finally, it so stirs the conscience of the opponent that reconciliation becomes a reality.

Sometimes you will read the literature of the student movement (against segregation) and see that, as they are getting ready for the sit-in or stand-in, they will read something like this: "If you are hit do not hit back, if you are cursed do not curse back." This is the whole idea, that the individual who is engaged in a nonviolent struggle must never inflict injury upon another.

I am convinced that the method of nonviolent resistance is the most potent weapon available to impress people in their struggle for freedom and human dignity. Therefore, I have advised all along that we follow a path of nonviolence, because, if we ever succumb to the temptation of using violence in our struggle, unborn generations will be the recipients of the long and desolate night of bitterness.

In a day when Sputniks and Explorers are slashing through outer space and guided ballistic missiles are carving highways of death, no nation can win a war. It is no longer the choice between violence and nonviolence; it is either nonviolence or nonexistence.

We will return good for evil. Christ showed us the way and Mahatma Gandhi showed us it could work.

We did not hesitate to call our (civil rights) movement an army. But it was a special army, with no supplies but its sincerity, no uniform but its determination, no arsenal except its faith, no currency but its conscience. It was an army that would move but not maul. It was an army that would sing but not slay. It was an army that would flank but not falter. It was an army to storm bastions of hatred, to lay siege to the fortresses of segregation, to surround symbols of discrimination. It was an army whose allegiance was to God and whose strategy and intelligence were the eloquently simple dictates of conscience.

Nonviolence had tremendous psychological importance to the Negro. He had to win and to vindicate his dignity in order to merit and enjoy his self-esteem. He had to let white men know that the picture of him as a clown—irresponsible, resigned and believing in his own inferiority—was a stereotype with no validity. This method was grasped by the Negro masses because it embodied the dignity of struggle, or moral conviction and self-sacrifice. The Negro was able to face his adversary, to concede to him a physical advantage and to defeat him because the superior force of the oppressor had become powerless.

Nonviolence, the answer to the Negro's need, may become the answer to the most desperate need of all humanity.

Nonviolence is a powerful and just weapon. It is a weapon unique in history, which cuts without wounding and ennobles the man who wields it. It is a sword that heals. Both a practical and a moral answer to the Negro's cry for justice, nonviolent direct action proved that it could win victories without losing wars.

To the Negro in 1963 . . . it had become obvious that nonviolence could symbolize the gold badge of heroism rather than the white feather of cowardice. In addition to being consistent with his religious precepts, it served his need to act on his own for his own liberation. It enabled him to transmute hatred into constructive energy, to seek not only to free himself but to free his oppressor from his sins. This transformation, in turn, had the marvelous effect of changing the face of the enemy. The enemy the Negro faced became not the individual who had oppressed him but the evil system which permitted that individual to do so.

Nonviolence is essentially a positive concept. Its corollary must always be growth. On the one hand nonviolence requires noncooperation with evil; on the other hand it requires cooperation with the constructive forces of good. Without this constructive aspect noncooperation ends where it begins.

The nonviolent approach does not immediately change the heart of the oppressor. It first does something to the hearts and souls of those committed to it. It gives them new self-respect; it calls up resources of strength and courage that they did not know they had. Finally it reaches the opponent and so stirs his conscience that reconciliation becomes a reality.

When, for decades, you have been able to make a man compromise his manhood by threatening him with a cruel and unjust punishment, and when suddenly he turns upon you and says: "Punish me. I do not deserve it. But because I do not deserve it, I will accept it so that the world will know that I am right and you are wrong," you hardly know what to do. You feel defeated and secretly ashamed. You know that this man is as good a man as you are; that from a mysterious source he has found the courage and the conviction to meet physical force with soul force.

If the philosophy of (nonviolence) had not emerged, by now many streets of the South would, I am convinced, be flowing with blood. And I am further convinced that if our white brothers dismiss as "rabble-rousers" and "outside agitators" those of us who employ nonviolent direct action, and if they refuse to support our nonviolent efforts, millions of Negroes will, out of frustration and despair, seek solace and security in black-nationalist ideologies—a development that would inevitably lead to a frightening racial nightmare.

. . . **Appeal to Conscience.** Nonviolence . . . is the method which seeks to implement the just law by appealing to the conscience of the great decent majority who through blindness, fear, pride, or irrationality have allowed their consciences to sleep.

. . . **Commitment.** Many Negroes are occupied in a middle-class struggle for status and prestige. They are more concerned about "conspicuous consumption" than about the cause of justice, and are probably not prepared for the ordeals and sacrifices involved in nonviolent action. Fortunately, however, the success of this method is not dependent on its unanimous acceptance. A few Negroes in every community, unswervingly committed to the nonviolent way, can persuade hundreds of others at least to use nonviolence as a technique and serve as the moral force to awaken the slumbering national conscience.

Mahatma Gandhi never had more than one hundred persons absolutely committed to his philosophy. But with this small group of devoted followers, he galvanized the whole of India, and through a magnificent feat of nonviolence challenged the might of the British Empire and won freedom for his people.

. . . **Love.** At the center of nonviolence stands the principle of love.

. . . **Reaction.** It is very important to see the difference between nonviolent demonstrations and riots. It may be true that in a demonstration people react with violence toward nonviolent demonstrators, but you don't blame the demonstrators. This would be like blaming the robbed man because his possession of money precipitated the evil act of robbery.

. . . **Suffering.** The way of nonviolence means a willingness to suffer and sacrifice. It may mean going to jail. If such is the case the resisters must be willing to fill the jail houses of the South. It may even mean physical death. But if physical death is the price that a man must pay to free his children and his white brethren from a permanent death of the spirit, then nothing could be more redemptive.

. . . **Universal.** The spiritual power that the Negro can radiate to the world comes from love, understanding, good will, and nonviolence. It may even be possible for the Negro, through adherence to nonviolence, so to challenge the nations of the world that they will seriously seek an alternative to war and destruction.

. . . **Versus Violence.** A mass movement of a militant quality that is not at the same time committed to nonviolence tends to generate conflict, which in turn breeds anarchy. The support of the participants and the sympathy of the uncommitted are both inhibited by the threat that bloodshed will engulf the community. This reaction in turn encourages the opposition to threaten and resort to force. When, however, the mass movement repudiates violence while moving resolutely toward its goal, its opponents are revealed as the instigators and practitioners of violence if it occurs. Then public support is magnetically attracted to the advocates of nonviolence, while those who employ violence are literally disarmed by overwhelming sentiment against their stand.

NONVIOLENT DIRECT ACTION

Our history teaches us that wielding the sword against racial superiority is not effective. The bravery of the Indian, employing spears and arrows against the Winchester and the Colt, had ultimately to eventuate in defeat. On the other hand, history also teaches that submission produces no acceptable result. Nonresistance merely reinforces the myth that one race is inherently inferior to another. Negroes today are neither exercising violence nor accepting domination. They are disturbing the tranquillity of the nation until the existence of injustice is recognized as a virulent disease menacing the whole society, and is cured. The Negro's method of nonviolent direct action is not only suitable as a remedy for injustice; its very nature is such that it challenges the myth of inferiority. Even the most reluctant are forced to recognize that no inferior people could choose and successfully pursue a course involving such extensive sacrifice, bravery and skill.

The Negro's weapon of nonviolent direct action is his only serviceable tool against injustice. He may be willing to sheath that sword but he has learned the wisdom of keeping it sharp.

In any nonviolent campaign there are four basic steps: collection of the facts to determine whether injustices are alive, negotiation, self-purification, and direct action.

Our demonstrations, boycotts, civil disobedience and political action in Negro-white unity won significant victories. In our judgment it remains the method that can succeed.

Nonviolent direct action seeks to create such a crisis and establish such creative tension that a community that has consistently refused to negotiate is forced to confront the issue. It seeks so to dramatize the issue that it can no longer be ignored.

. . . **Discipline.** There must be, always, in a nonviolent movement, a sense of political timing. I do not believe in the indiscriminate use of any form of demonstration. I think we must be well disciplined and think through our moves, and we must clearly define our goals.

NONVIOLENT RESISTANCE

Nehru once remarked that the British were never so angry as when the Indians resisted them with nonviolence, that he never saw eyes so full of hate as those of the British troops to whom he turned the other cheek when they beat him with lathis. But nonviolent resistance at least changed the minds and hearts of the Indians, however impervious the British may have appeared. "We cast away our fear," says Nehru. And in the end the British not only granted freedom to India but came to have a new respect for the Indians. Today a mutual friendship based on complete equality exists between these two peoples within the Commonwealth.

The nonviolent resister is willing to accept violence if necessary, but never to inflict it.

The Christian doctrine of love operating through the Gandhian method of nonviolence was one of the most potent weapons available to the Negro in his struggle for freedom.

Nonviolent resistance paralyzed and confused the power structures against which it was directed. The brutality with which officials would have quelled the black individual became impotent when it could not be pursued with stealth and remain unobserved. It was caught—as a fugitive from a penitentiary is often caught—in gigantic circling spotlights. It was imprisoned in a luminous glare revealing the naked truth to the whole world.

NORTH AND SOUTH

Few people in America realize the seriousness of the burden imposed upon our democracy by the disenfranchisement of

Negroes in the Deep South. . . . This has led to a serious crisis not only for the Negro in the South but for Negroes in the swollen ghettos of the North. Northern cities are inheriting the results of northern indifference to southern racism and exploitation as the victims of oppression migrate there in search of freedom.

OLD GUARD

The old guard in any society resents new methods, for old guards wear the decorations and medals won by waging battle in the accepted manner.

OPENMINDEDNESS

The call for intelligence is a call for open-mindedness, sound judgment, and love for truth. It is a call for men to rise above the stagnation of closed-mindedness and the paralysis of gullibility. One does not need to be a profound scholar to be open-minded, nor a keen academician to engage in an assiduous pursuit for truth.

OPPORTUNITY

Place your failure at the forefront of your mind and stare daringly at it. Ask yourself, "How may I transform this liability into an asset?" . . . Almost anything that happens to us may be woven into the purposes of God. It may lengthen our cords of sympathy. It may break our self-centered pride. The cross, which was willed by wicked men, was woven by God into the tapestry of world redemption.

OPPRESSION

When oppressed people willingly accept their oppression they only serve to give the oppressor a convenient justification for his acts. Often the oppressor goes along unaware of the evil involved in his oppression so long as the oppressed accepts it. So in order to be true to one's conscience and true to God, a righteous man has no alternative but to refuse to cooperate with an evil system.

The oppressed must never allow the conscience of the oppressor to slumber.

History reveals to us that once oppressed people rise up against that oppression, there is no stopping point short of full freedom.

. . . **Apathy.** In every movement toward freedom some of the oppressed prefer to remain oppressed. Almost 2800 years ago Moses set out to lead the children of Israel from the slavery of Egypt to the freedom of the promised land. He soon discovered that slaves do not always welcome their deliverers. They become accustomed to being slaves. They would rather bear those ills they have, as Shakespeare pointed out, than flee to others that they know not of. They prefer the "fleshpots of Egypt" to the ordeals of emancipation.

. . . **Duty of Oppressed.** Religion reminds every man that he is his brother's keeper. To accept injustice or segregation passively is to say to the oppressor that his actions are morally right. It is a way of allowing his conscience to fall asleep. At this moment the oppressed fails to be his brother's keeper.

To accept passively an unjust system is to cooperate with that system; thereby the oppressed become as evil as the oppressor. Noncooperation with evil is as much a moral obligation as is cooperation with good.

. . . **Resignation.** There is such a thing as the freedom of exhaustion. Some people are so worn down by the yoke of oppression that they give up. A few years ago in the slum areas of Atlanta, a Negro guitarist used to sing almost daily: "Been down so long that down don't bother me." This is the type of negative freedom and resignation that often engulfs the life of the oppressed.

· · P · ·

PACIFISM

True pacifism is not nonresistance to evil, but nonviolent resistance to evil.

True pacifism is not unrealistic submission to evil power. . . . It is rather a courageous confrontation of evil by the power of love, in the faith that it is better to be the recipient of violence than the inflicter of it, since the latter only multiplies the existence of violence and bitterness in the universe, while the former may develop a sense of shame in the opponent, and thereby bring about a transformation and change of heart.

The pacifist would have a greater appeal if he did not claim to be free from the moral dilemma that the Christian nonpacifist confronts.

I came to see the pacifist position not as sinless but as the lesser evil in the circumstances.

PARTICIPATION

As the broadcasting profession will confirm, no shows are so successful as those which allow for audience participation. In order to be somebody, people must feel themselves part of something. In the nonviolent army, there is room for everyone who wants to join up. There is no color distinction. There is no examination, no pledge, except that, as a soldier in the armies of violence is expected to inspect his carbine and keep it clean, nonviolent soldiers are called upon to examine and burnish their greatest weapons—their heart, their conscience, their courage and their sense of justice.

PASSIVE RESISTANCE

Wherever segregation exists we must be willing to rise up

in mass and protest courageously against it. I realize that this type of courage means suffering and sacrifice. It might mean going to jail. If such is the case we must honorably fill up the jailhouses of the South. It might even lead to physical death. But if such physical death is the price that we must pay to free our children from a life of permanent psychological death, then nothing could be more honorable. This is really the meaning of the method of passive resistance. It confronts physical force with an even stronger force, namely, soul force.

PEACE

True peace is not merely the absence of tension, but it is the presence of justice and brotherhood.

Those of us who love peace must organize as effectively as the war hawks.

We must use our minds as rigorously to plan for peace as we have used them to plan for war.

True peace is not merely the absence of some negative force—tension, confusion or war; it is the presence of some positive force—justice, good will and brotherhood.

Sooner or later, all the people of the world will have to discover a way to live together in peace, and thereby transform this pending cosmic elegy into a creative psalm of brotherhood.

Through the vistas of time a voice still cries to every potential Peter, "Put up your sword!" The shores of history are white with the bleachèd bones of nations and communities that failed to follow this command.

PEACE CORPS

The Peace Corps will fail if it seeks to do something *for* the underprivileged peoples of the world; it will succeed if it seeks creatively to do something *with* them. It will fail as a negative gesture to defeat Communism; it will succeed only as a positive effort to wipe poverty, ignorance, and disease from the earth.

PERSONALITY

Looking at each other, we quickly conclude that our perception of the physical body is a vision of all that we are. . . . (But) you can never see the *me* that makes me me, and I can never see the *you* that makes you you. That invisible something we call personality is beyond our physical gaze. Plato was right when he said that the visible is a shadow cast by the invisible.

The strong man holds in a living blend strongly marked opposites. Not ordinarily do men achieve this balance of opposites. The idealists are not usually realistic, and the realists are not usually idealistic. The militant are not generally known to be passive, nor the passive to be militant. Seldom are the humble self-assertive, or the self-assertive humble. But life at its best is a creative synthesis of opposites in fruitful harmony.

It is certainly true that human personality is limited, but personality as such involves no necessary limitations. It means simply self-consciousness and self-direction.

POLITICS

If we can get a sizable number of Negro voters, we will be able to change the structure of politics in this country.

. . . **Blocs.** (Political) blocs are not unique in American life, nor are they inherently evil. Their purposes determine their moral quality. In past years, labor, farmers, businessmen, veterans, and various national minorities have voted as blocs on various issues, and many still do. If the objectives are good, and each issue is decided on its own merits, a bloc is a wholesome force on the political scene.

Effectiveness is the aim of bloc voting; by forming a bloc a minority makes its voice heard. The Negro minority will unite for political action for the same reason that it will seek to function in alliance with other groups—because in this way it can compel the majority to listen.

. . . **Conscience.** I feel that someone must remain in the position of (political) nonalignment, so that he can look objectively at both parties and be the conscience of both—not the servant or master of either.

. . . **Negroes.** The Negro potential for political power is now substantial. Negroes are strategically situated in large cities, especially in the North but also in the South, and these cities in turn are decisive in state elections. These same states are the key in a Presidential race, and frequently determine the nomination. This unique factor gives Negroes enormous leverage in the balance of power.

Because Negroes can quite readily become a compact, conscious and vigorous force in politics, they can do more than achieve their own racial goals. American politics needs nothing so much as an injection of the idealism, self-sacrifice and sense of public service which is the hallmark of our movement.

Political power may well, in the days to come, be the most effective new tool of the Negro's liberation.

Negroes have traditionally positioned themselves too far from the inner arena of political decision. Few other minority groups have maintained a political aloofness and a nonpartisan posture as rigidly and as long as Negroes. The Germans, Irish, Italians, and Jews, after a period of acclimatization, moved inside political formations and exercised influence. Negroes, partly by choice but substantially by exclusion, have operated outside of the political structures, functioning instead essentially as a pressure group with limited effect.

Political leaders are infinitely respectful toward any group that has an abundance of energy to ring doorbells, man the street corners and escort voters to the polls. Negroes in their demonstrations and voter-registration campaigns have been acquiring excellent training in just these tasks. They also have discipline perhaps beyond that of any other group, because it has become a condition of survival. Consider the political power that would be generated if the million Americans who marched in 1963 also put their energy directly into the electoral process.

. . . **Negro Voting.** The more we gain the (voting) right and utilize the right after we gain it, the more we will see a change in the total political structure of the South. This in a sense will give us a change in the political structure and the political climate of our whole nation, because we still know that in Congress many of our most important committees are held by southern racists. They are chairmen of these committees and they can still block important legislation. Therefore, the right to vote for the Negro in the South will do many things. That it will liberalize the total political climate, I am absolutely convinced.

. . . **South.** Congress today is dominated by southern reactionaries whose control of the key committees enables them to determine legislation. Disenfranchisement of the Negro and the nonexercise of the vote by poor whites have permitted the southern congressman to wrest his election from a tiny group, which he manipulates easily to return him again and again to office. United with northern reactionaries, these unrepresentative legislators have crippled the country by blocking urgently needed action. Only with the growth of an enlightened electorate, white and Negro together, can we put a quick end to this century-old stranglehold of a minority on the nation's legislative processes.

POSITIVISM

We must not call everyone a Communist or an appeaser who recognizes that hate and hysteria are not the final answers to the problems of these turbulent days. We must not engage in a negative anti-Communism, but rather in a positive thrust for democracy, realizing that our greatest defense against Communism is to take offensive action in behalf of justice and righteousness.

POTENTIALITY

Potential powers of creativity are within us, and we have the duty to work assiduously to discover these powers.

POVERTY

Our nation is now so rich, productive, that the continuation of persistent poverty is incendiary because the poor cannot rationalize their deprivation.

The apathy from which Negroes suffered for so long was derived from their powerlessness and their acceptance of the myth that abundance was not available. They are now accumulating power; they are taught by every media of communication that we are so opulent we can enjoy both butter and guns.

We have yet to confront and solve the international problems created by our wealth in a world still largely hungry and miserable. But more immediate and pressing is the domestic existence of poverty. It is an anachronism in the second half of the twentieth century. Only the neglect to plan intelligently and adequately and the unwillingness genuinely to embrace economic justice enable it to persist.

Poverty—especially that found among 35 million persons in the United States—is rooted not in a lack of resources, but in a tragic defect of human will.

The inseparable twin of racial unjustice is economic injustice. . . . The systems of segregation exploit both the Negro and the poor whites.

God never intended one people to live in superfluous and inordinate wealth, while others know only deadening poverty. God wants all of his children to have the basic necessities of life, and he has left in this universe "enough and to spare" for that purpose.

. . . **Race Prejudice.** Not logic but a hollow social distinction has separated the races. The economically depressed white accepts his poverty by telling himself that, if in no other respect, at least socially he is above the Negro. For this empty pride in a racial myth he has paid the crushing price of insecurity, hunger, ignorance, and hoplessness for himself and his children.

. . . **Unemployment.** Unemployment is a form of brutality, especially violent for those who live on the edge of poverty.

POVERTY AID

I am proposing . . . that, just as we granted a GI Bill of Rights to war veterans, America launch a broadbased and gigantic Bill of Rights for the Disadvantaged, our veterans of the long siege of denial.

A Bill of Rights for the Disadvantaged could mark the rise of a new era, in which the full resources of the society would be used to attack the tenacious poverty which so paradoxically exists in the midst of plenty.

POWER

A mass movement exercising nonviolence is an object lesson in power under discipline, a demonstration to the white community that if such a movement attained a degree of strength, it would use its power creatively and not vengefully.

There is a creative power that works to pull down mountains of evil and level hilltops of injustice.

PRAYER AND ACTION

God, who gave us minds for thinking and bodies for working, would defeat his own purpose if he permitted us to obtain through prayer what may come through work and intelligence. Prayer is a marvelous and necessary supplement of our feeble efforts, but it is a dangerous substitute.

I am certain we need to pray for God's help and guidance in this integration struggle, but we are gravely misled if we think the struggle will be won only by prayer.

We must pray with unceasing passion for racial justice, but we must also use our minds to develop a program, organize ourselves into mass nonviolent action, and employ every resource of our bodies and souls to bring an end to racial injustice. We must pray unrelentingly for economic justice, but we must also work diligently to bring into being those social changes that make for a better distribution of wealth within our nation and in the undeveloped countries of the world.

PREJUDICE

Many people in the North have come to realize that they probably had much more deep-seated prejudices than they had been conscious of. It took the big push by the Negro community and the allies of the Negro in the white community to bring this whole issue to the surface in 1963. . . . It's something like a boil, which, if kept covered up, will never be cured. It's only when you open it to air and light that it can be cured, even though it's ugly for the moment.

. . . **Ignorance.** Softmindedness is one of the basic causes of race prejudice. The toughminded person always examines the facts before he reaches conclusions; in short, he postjudges. The tenderminded person reaches a conclusion before he has examined the first fact; in short, he prejudges and is prejudiced.

PRESIDENCY

Legislative enactments, like court decisions, declare rights, but do not automatically deliver them. Ultimately, Executive action determines what force and effect legislation will have.

The President is the embodiment of the democratic personality of the nation, both domestically and internationally. His own personal conduct influences and educates.

. . . **Responsibility.** The executive heads of our nation must not wait for some great crisis to emerge before asserting forthright action, but must make it palpably clear on a day-to-day basis that their power, their moral leadership and authority, are committed to the task of removing the ugly weight of racial discrimination from the shoulders of the nation.

PRESS

It is terribly difficult to wage . . . a battle without the moral support of the national press to counteract the hostility of local editors.

PRESSURE

You cannot depend upon American institutions to function without pressure.

PRISON

God's companionship does not stop at the door of a jail cell.

When we speak of filling the jails, we are talking of a tactic to be flexibly applied. No responsible person would promise to fill all jails everywhere at any time. Leaders indulge in bombast if they do not take all circumstances into account before calling upon their people to make a maximum sacrifice. Filling jails means that thousands of people must leave their jobs, perhaps to lose them, put off responsibilities, undergo harrowing psychological experiences for which law-abiding people are not routinely prepared.

PRIVILEGE

History is the long and tragic story of the fact that privileged groups seldom give up their privileges voluntarily.

No one gives up his privileges without strong resistance.

PROFITS

The profit motive, when it is the sole basis of an economic system, encourages a cutthroat competition and selfish ambition that inspires men to be more concerned about making a living than making a life.

PROGRESS

Human progress is neither automatic nor inevitable.

Human progress never rolls in on wheels of inevitability; it comes through the tireless efforts of man willing to be coworkers with God, and without this hard work, time itself becomes an ally of the forces of social stagnation.

Even a superficial look at history reveals that no social advance rolls in on the wheels of inevitability. Every step toward the goal of justice requires sacrifice, suffering, and struggle; the tireless exertions and passionate concern of dedicated individuals.

All progress is precarious, and the solution of one problem brings us face to face with another problem.

. . . **Striving.** Even though all progress is precarious, within limits real social progress may be made. Although man's moral pilgrimage may never reach a destination point on earth, his never-ceasing strivings may bring him ever closer to the city of righteousness.

PROTEST

Certainly we all want to live the well-adjusted life in order to avoid neurotic and schizophrenic personalities. But I must honestly say . . . that there are some things in our nation and in our world of which I am proud to be maladjusted. I call upon all men of good will to be maladjusted until the good society is realized. I . . . never intend to adjust myself to segregation and discrimination. I never intend to become adjusted to religious bigotry. I never intend to adjust myself to madness of militarism and the self-defeating effects of physical violence.

To cooperate passively with an unjust system makes the oppressed as evil as the oppressor.

PUBLICITY

Only the shallow-minded are excited over publicity. Publicity is evanescent; it is here today and gone tomorrow. . . . Whoever falls in love with publicity is not fit to have it and will end up in misery.

PUBLIC OPINION

Public opinion (is) not in a rigid mold. American political thought (is) not committed to conservatism, nor radicalism, nor moderation. It (is) above all fluid. As such it contains trends rather than hard lines, and affirmative leadership (can) guide it into constructive channels.

QUALITY

. . . **Versus Quantity.** We must not be tempted to confuse spiritual power and large numbers. Jumboism, as someone has called it, is an utterly fallacious standard for measuring positive power. An increase in quantity does not automatically bring an increase in quality. A larger (church) membership does not necessarily represent a correspondingly increased commitment to Christ.

··R··

RACE

The idea of an inferior or superior race has been refuted by the best evidence of the science of anthropology. Great anthropologists, like Ruth Benedict, Margaret Mead, and Melville J. Herskovits, agree that, although there may be inferior and superior individuals within all races, there is no superior or inferior race.

In the final analysis the problem of race is not a political but a moral issue.

RACE PREJUDICE

. . . **North and South.** The strait jackets of race prejudice and discrimination do not wear only southern labels. The subtle, psychological technique of the North has approached in its ugliness and victimization of the Negro the outright terror and open brutality of the South.

RACIAL CRISIS

The rumblings of discontent in Asia and Africa are expressions of a quest for freedom and human dignity by people who have long been the victims of colonialism and imperialism. So in a real sense the racial crisis in America is a part of the larger world crisis.

In the present crisis America can achieve either racial justice or the ultimate social psychosis that can only lead to domestic suicide. The democratic ideal of freedom and equality will be fulfilled for all—or all human beings will share in the resulting social and spiritual doom. In short, this crisis has the potential for democracy's fulfillment or fascism's triumph; for social progress or retrogression. We can choose either to walk the high road of human brotherhood or to tread the low road of man's inhumanity to man.

RACIAL DISCRIMINATION

The federal government collects taxes from all citizens, Negro and white, which it is Constitutionally obligated to use for the benefit of all; yet billions of these tax dollars have gone to support housing programs and hospital and airport construction in which discrimination is an open and notorious practice.

RACIAL JUSTICE

Anyone sensitive to the present moods, morals and trends in our nation must know that the time for racial justice has come. The issue is not *whether* segregation and discrimination will be eliminated, but *how* they will pass from the scene.

Anyone who starts out with the conviction that the road to racial justice is only one lane wide will inevitably create a traffic jam and make the journey infinitely longer.

RACISM

Christianity repudiates racism.

Numerous people in the North and South still believe that the affirmation "All men are created equal" means "All white men are created equal."

RATIONALIZATION

It seems to be a fact of life that human nature cannot continue to do wrong without eventually reaching out for some rationalization which will help to clothe an obvious wrong in the beautiful garments of righteousness.

REASON

By his ability to reason, his power of memory, and his gift

of imagination, man transcends time and space. As marvelous as are the stars is the mind of man that studies them.

REASON VERSUS EMOTION

Dictators, capitalizing on softmindedness, have led men to acts of barbarity and terror that are unthinkable in civilized society. Adolf Hitler realized that softmindedness was so prevalent among his followers that he said, "I use emotion for the many and reserve reason for the few."

REFORMERS

Someone has said, "I love reforms but I hate reformers." A reformer may be an untransformed nonconformist whose rebellion against the evils of society has left him annoyingly rigid and unreasonably impatient.

RELIGION

For so many Christians, Christianity is a Sunday activity having no relevancy for Monday and the church is little more than a secular social club having a thin veneer of religiosity. Jesus is an ancient symbol whom we do the honor of calling Christ, and yet his Lordship is neither affirmed nor acknowledged by our substantive lives. Would that the Christian fire were burning in the hearts of all Christians with the same intensity as the Communist fire is burning in the hearts of Communists! Is Communism alive in the world today because we have not been Christian enough?

Otherworldly concerns have a deep and significant place in all religions worthy of the name. Any religion that is completely earthbound sells its birthright for a mess of naturalistic pottage. Religion, at its best, deals not only with man's preliminary concerns but with his inescapable ultimate concern. When religion overlooks this basic fact it is reduced to a mere ethical system in which eternity is absorbed into time and God is relegated to a sort of meaningless figment of the human imagination.

. . . and Ignorance. Religion has sometimes rejected new truth with a dogmatic passion. Through edicts and bulls, inquisitions and excommunications, the church has attempted to prorogue truth and place an impenetrable stone wall in the path of the truth-seeker. The historical-philological criticism of the Bible is considered by the softminded as blasphemous, and reason is often looked upon as the exercise of a corrupt faculty. Softminded persons have revised the Beatitudes to read, "Blessed are the pure in ignorance: for they shall see God."

. . . Poverty. Religion at its best realizes that the soul is crushed as long as the body is tortured with hunger pangs and harrowed with the need for shelter.

. . . Social Concern. Only a "dry as dust" religion prompts a minister to extol the glories of Heaven while ignoring the social conditions that cause men an earthly hell.

By ignoring the need for social reform, religion is divorced from the mainstream of human life. A pulpit committee listed as the first essential qualification for a new minister: "He must preach the true gospel and not talk about social issues." This is a blueprint for a dangerously irrelevant church where people assemble to hear only pious platitudes.

RELIGION AND SCIENCE

There may be a conflict between softminded religionists and toughminded scientists, but not between science and religion. Their respective worlds are different and their methods are dissimilar. Science investigates; religion interprets. Science gives man knowledge which is power; religion gives man wisdom which is control. Science deals mainly with facts; religion deals mainly with values. The two are not rivals. They are complementary. Science keeps religion from sinking into the valley of crippling irrationalism and paralyzing obscurantism. Religion prevents science from falling into the marsh of obsolete materialism and moral nihilism.

RESENTMENTS

Medical science reveals that such physical ailments as arthritis, gastric ulcer, and asthma have on occasion been encouraged by bitter resentments. Psychosomatic medicine, dealing with bodily sicknesses which come from mental illnesses, shows how deep resentment may result in physical deterioration.

RESOURCES

All too many people attempt to face the tensions of life with inadequate spiritual resources. When vacationing in Mexico, Mrs. King and I wished to go deep-sea fishing. For reasons of economy, we rented an old and poorly equipped boat. We gave this little thought until, ten miles from shore, the clouds lowered and howling winds blew. Then we became paralyzed with fear, for we knew our boat was deficient. Multitudes of people are in a similar situation. Heavy winds and weak boats explain their fear.

RETALIATION

A guilt-ridden white minority fears that if the Negro attains power, he will without restraint or pity act to revenge the accumulated injustices and brutality of the years. A parent, who has continually mistreated his son, suddenly realizes that he is now taller than the parent. Will the son use his new physical power to repay for all the blows of the past?

The strong man is the man who can stand up for his rights and does not hit back.

The nonviolent resister would contend that in the struggle for human dignity, the oppressed people of the world must not succumb to the temptation of becoming bitter or indulging in hate campaigns. To retaliate in kind would do nothing but intensify the existence of hate in the universe. Along the way of life, someone must have sense enough and morality enough to cut off the chain of hate. This can only be done by projecting the ethic of love to the center of our lives.

We live according to the philosophy that life is a matter of getting even and of saving face. We bow before the altar of revenge. Samson, eyeless at Gaza, prays fervently for his enemies—but only for their utter destruction. The potential beauty of human life is constantly made ugly by man's ever-recurring song of retaliation.

REVENGE

The oceans of history are made turbulent by the ever-rising tides of revenge. Man has never risen above the injunction of the *lex talionis:* "Life for life, eye for eye, tooth for tooth, hand for hand, foot for foot." In spite of the fact that the law of revenge solves no social problems, men continue to follow its disastrous leading. History is cluttered with the wreckage of nations and individuals that pursued this self-defeating path.

The old law of an eye for an eye leaves everybody blind.

REVOLUTION

No revolution is executed like a ballet. Its steps and gestures are not neatly designed and precisely performed.

With initial success, every social revolution simultaneously does two things: It attracts to itself fresh forces and strength, and at the same time it crystallizes the opposition.

Some believe that (the Negro Revolution) is the work of skilled agitators who have the power to raise or lower the floodgates at will. Such a movement, maneuverable by a talented few, would not be a genuine revolution.

A social movement that only moves people is merely a revolt. A movement that changes both people and institutions is a revolution.

RIGHT

We proved . . . (in Birmingham, Alabama) that we needed

no weapons—not so much as a toothpick. We proved that we possessed the most formidable weapon of all—the conviction that we were right. We had the protection of our knowledge that we were more concerned about realizing our righteous aims than about saving our skins.

RIOTS

I think demonstrations must continue, but I think riots must end, because I think they are socially disruptive.

· · S · ·

SCHOOL DESEGRATION

The phrase "all deliberate speed" (in the Supreme Court school desegregation decision) did not mean that another century should be allowed to unfold before we released Negro children from the narrow pigeonhole of the segregated schools; it meant that, giving some courtesy and consideration to the need for softening old attitudes and outdated customs, democracy must press ahead, out of the past of ignorance and intolerance, and into the present of educational opportunity and moral freedom.

The Negro had been deeply disappointed over the slow pace of school desegregation. He knew that in 1954 the highest court in the land had handed down a decree calling for desegregation of schools "with all deliberate speed." He knew that this edict from the Supreme Court had been heeded with all deliberate delay.

SCIENCE

The devotees of the new man-centered religion point to the spectacular advances of modern science as justification for their faith. . . . But alas! something has shaken the faith of those who have made the laboratory "the new cathedral of men's hopes." The instruments which yesterday were worshiped today contain cosmic death, threatening to plunge all of us into the abyss of annihilation. Man is not able to save himself or the world.

Science can give us only physical power, which, if not controlled by spiritual power, will lead inevitably to cosmic doom. The words of Alfred the Great are still true: "Power is never a good unless he be good that has it." We need something more spiritually sustainmg and morally controlling than science. It is an instrument which, under the power of God's spirit, may lead man to greater heights of physical security, but apart from Gods' spirit, science is a deadly weapon that will lead only to deeper chaos.

SCIENCE AND GOD

Our man-made instruments seem barely to be moving in comparison to the movement of the God-created solar system. Think about the fact, for instance, that the earth is circling the sun so fast that the fastest jet would be left sixty-six thousand miles behind in the first hour of a space race.

SECOND-CLASS CITIZENSHIP

The long-deferred issue of second-class citizenship has become our nation's first-class crisis. We can deal with it now, or we can drive a seething humanity to a desperation it tried, asked and hoped to avoid.

SECULARISM

Most men do not say, "Good-by, God, I am going to leave you now." But they become so involved in the things of this world that they are unconsciously carried away by the rushing tide of materialism and are left treading in the confused waters of secularism.

SEGREGATION

(Segregationists) probably think they are right in their methods of dealing with Negroes. They say the things they say about us and treat us as they do because they have been taught these things. From the cradle to the grave, it is instilled in them that the Negro is inferior. Their parents probably taught them that; the schools they attended taught them that; the books they read, even their ·churches and ministers, often taught them that; and above all the very concept of segregation teaches them that. The whole cultural tradition under which they have grown—a tradition blighted with more than 250 years of slavery and more than 90 years of segregation—teaches them that Negroes do not deserve certain things. So these men are merely the children of their culture. When they seek to preserve segregation they are seeking to preserve only what their local folkways have taught them was right.

(A) basic force at work (among Negroes) was their corroding sense of inferiority, which often expressed itself in a lack of self-respect. Many unconsciously wondered whether they actually deserved any better conditions. Their minds and souls were so conditioned to the system of segregation that they submissively adjusted themselves to things as they were. This is the ultimate tragedy of segregation. It not only harms one physically but injures one spiritually. It scars the soul and degrades the personality. It inflicts the segregated with a false sense of inferiority, while confirming the segregator in a false estimate of his own superiority. It is a system which forever stares the segregated in the face, saying: "You are less than . . ." "You are not equal to . . ."

We have waited for more than three hundred and forty years for our God-given and constitutional rights. The nations of Asia and Africa are moving with jetlike speed toward the goal of political independence, and we still creep at horse-and-buggy pace toward the gaining of a cup of coffee at a lunch counter.

We have waited for more than three hundred and forty years for our Constitutional and God-given rights. . . . I guess it is easy for those who have never felt the stinging darts of segregation to say "wait." . . . But when you find it necessary to sleep night after night in the uncomfortable corners of your automobile because no motel will accept you; when you are humiliated day in and day out by nagging signs reading "white" men and "colored," when your first name becomes "nigger" and your middle name becomes "boy" (however old you are) and your last name becomes "John," and when your wife and mother are never given the respected title "Mrs."; when you are harried by day and haunted by night by the fact that you are a Negro, living constantly at tiptoe stance . . . and plagued with inner fears and outer resentments; when you are forever fighting a degenerating sense of "nobodiness"—then you will understand why we find it difficult to wait.

I could never adjust to the separate waiting rooms, separate eating places, separate rest rooms, partly because the separate was always unequal, and partly because the very idea of separation did something to my sense of dignity and self-respect.

I remember riding with my father one day when he accidentally drove past a stop sign. A policeman pulled up to the car and said: "All right, boy, pull over and let me see your license." My father replied indignantly, "I'm no boy." Then, pointing to me, "This is a boy. I'm a man, and until you call me one, I will not listen to you." The policeman was so shocked that he wrote the ticket up nervously, and left the scene as quickly as possible.

The Negro's struggle for complete emancipation and full citizenship has been met at each step by the same distinct pattern of resistance, with only the weapons changing from lynching, violence and intimidation to restrictive covenants, black codes, Jim Crow laws, to avoidance, interposition, nullification, and now even open contempt.

The problem of racial injustice will not work itself out. It means hard work.

I considered segregation both rationally inexplicable and morally unjustifiable. I could never accept my having to sit in the back of a bus or in the segregated section of a train. The first time that I was seated behind a curtain in a dining car I felt as though the curtain had been dropped on my selfhood.

Segregation has been the Negro's burden and America's shame.

Segregation distorts the soul and damages the personality. It gives the segregator a false sense of superiority and the segregated a false sense of inferiority. Segregation, to use the terminology of the Jewish philosopher Martin Buber, substitutes an "I-it" relationship for an "I-thou" relationship and ends up relegating persons to the status of things. Hence segregation is not only politically, economically and sociologically unsound, it is morally wrong and sinful.

Segregation . . . is a stench in the nostrils of almighty God.

Thousands of Negroes have come to see that it is ultimately more honorable to suffer in dignity than to accept segregation in humiliation.

It is true that segregation is on its deathbed. But history has proven that social systems have a great last-minute breathing power. And the guardians of the status quo are always on hand with their oxygen tents to preserve the dying order.

The underlying philosophy of democracy is diametrically opposed to the underlying philosophy of segregation, and all the dialectics of logicians cannot make them lie down together. Segregation is a cancer in the body politic which must be removed before our democratic health can be realized.

The whole rotten, ugly system of racial injustice for 350 years has degraded the doer as well as the victim.

We will make progress if we accept the fact that four hundred years of sinning cannot be canceled out in four minutes of atonement. Neither can we allow the guilty to tailor their atonement in such a manner as to visit another four seconds of deliberate hurt upon the victims.

Even the segregationists know: The system to which they have been committed lies on its deathbed. The only imponderable is the question of how costly they will make the funeral.

The Negro is not ready for integration, they say; because of academic and cultural lags on the part of the Negro, the integration of schools will pull the white race down. They are never honest enough to admit that the academic and cultural lags in the Negro community are themselves the result of segregation and discrimination. The best way to solve any problem is to remove its cause. It is both rationally unsound and sociologically untenable to use the tragic effects of segregation as an argument for its continuation.

Justice and equality . . . would never come while segregation remained, because the basic purpose of segregation was to perpetuate injustice and inequality.

. . . **America.** Segregation is still a fact in America. We still confront it in the South in its glaring and conspicuous forms. We still confront it in the North in its hidden and subtle forms. But if democracy is to live, segregation must die.

. . . **Armed Forces.** It is ironic that, for so many years, the armed forces of this nation, even in time of war, were prisoners of the southern system of segregation. The military establishment could tear a man away from his wife and child, and reorient, within weeks, his entire mode of life and conduct. But not until World War II did the Army begin to conceive that it had the right, the obligation and the ability to say that a white man in uniform must respect the dignity of a black man in uniform.

. . . **Bible.** There are Christians . . . who try to find biblical bases to justify segregation and argue that the Negro is inferior by nature. . . . This is blasphemy and against everything that the Christian religion stands for.

. . . **Biblical Justification.** It was argued from pulpits that Negroes were inferior by nature because of Noah's curse upon the children of Ham. Paul's command, "Servant, be obedient to your master," became a watchword. One parson could state in terms almost comparable to an Aristotelian syllogism, "Man is made in the image of God; God, as everybody knows, is not a Negro, therefore, the Negro is not a man."

. . . **Children.** Every parent at some time faces the problem of explaining the facts of life to his child. Just as inevitably, for the Negro parent, the moment comes when he must explain to his offspring the facts of segregation. My mother took me on her lap and began by telling me about slavery and how it had ended with the Civil War. She tried to explain the divided system of the South—the segregated schools, restaurants, theaters, housing; the white and colored signs on drinking fountains, waiting rooms, lavatories—as a social condition rather than a natural order. Then she said the words that almost every Negro hears before he can yet understand the injustice that makes them necessary: "You are as good as anyone."

. . . **Fear.** Racial segregation is buttressed by such irrational fears as loss of preferred economic privilege, altered social status, intermarriage, and adjustment to new situations. Through sleepless nights and haggard days numerous white people attempt to combat these corroding fears by diverse methods. By following the path of escape, some seek to ignore the question of race relations and to close their mind to the issues involved. Others, placing their faith in such legal maneuvers as interposition and nullification, counsel massive resistance. Still others hope to drown their fear by engaging in acts of violence and meanness toward their Negro brethren. But how futile are all these remedies! Instead of eliminating fear, they instill deeper and more pathological fears that leave the victims inflicted with strange psychoses and peculiar cases of paranoia.

. . . **Legal.** Segregation has so often been a legal fact in the South and therefore we have had this overt expression of the problem. In the North in many instances it is covert, it is more subtle. It is a little more *de facto* than *de jure*. It is *de facto* segregation, for instance, that we see in many areas of the North where certainly it doesn't have the sanction of the law.

. . . **North and South.** Segregation may exist in the South in overt ingrained forms, but it exists in the North in hidden and subtle ways. Discrimination in housing and employment is often as bad in the North as it is anywhere. The racial crisis confronting America is not a sectional issue but a national problem.

. . . **Oppression.** The underlying purpose of segregation was to oppress and exploit the segregated, not simply to keep them apart.

. . . **Politics.** The President has proposed a ten-year plan to put a man on the moon. We do not yet have a plan to put a Negro in the State Legislature of Alabama.

. . . **Slavery.** Segregation is nothing but slavery covered up with certain niceties of complexity.

. . . **Social and Economic.** Negroes are still at the bottom of the economic ladder. They live within two concentric circles of segregation. One imprisons them on the basis of color, while the other confines them within a separate culture of poverty. The average Negro is born into want and deprivation. His struggle to escape his circumstances is hindered by color discrimination. He is deprived of normal education and normal social and economic opportunities. When he seeks opportunity, he is told, in effect, to lift himself by his own bootstraps, advice which does not take into account the fact that he is barefoot.

. . . **South.** The basic institutions of government, commerce, industry and social patterns in the South all rest upon the embedded institutions of segregation.

SEGREGATION AND COLONIALISM

There is no basic difference between colonialism and racial segregation, although naturally there are surface differences.

SELF-CONCERN

If an American is concerned only about his nation, he will not be concerned about the peoples of Asia, Africa, or South America. Is this not why nations engage in the madness of war without the slightest sense of penitence? Is this not why the murder of a citizen of your own nation is a crime, but the murder of the citizens of another nation in war is an act of heroic virtue? If manufacturers are concerned only in their personal interests, they will pass by on the other side while thousands of working people are stripped of their jobs and left displaced on some Jericho Road as a result of automation, and they will judge every move toward a better distribution of wealth and a better life for the working man to be socialistic.

SELFISHNESS

Social psychologists tell us that we cannot truly be persons unless we interact with other persons. All life is interrelated, and all men are interdependent. And yet we continue to travel a road paved with the slippery cement of inordinate selfishness.

SEPARATION

Men often hate each other because they fear each other; they fear each other because they do not know each other; they do not know each other because they cannot communicate; they cannot communicate because they are separated.

SERMONS

A sermon is not an essay to be read but a discourse to be heard.

SERVITUDE

The old order ends, no matter what Bastilles remain, when the enslaved within themselves, bury the psychology of servitude.

SIN

The more I observed the tragedies of history and man's shameful inclination to choose the low road, the more I came to see the depths and strength of sin.

The superficial optimism of liberalism concerning human nature overlooked the fact that reason is darkened by sin. The more I thought about human nature, the more I saw how our tragic inclination for sin encourages us to rationalize our actions. Liberalism failed to show that reason by itself is little more than an instrument to justify man's defensive ways of thinking. Reason, devoid of the purifying power of faith, can never free itself from distortions and rationalizations.

We err when we assume that because man is made in the

image of God, man is basically good. Through his all too prevalent inclination for evil, man has terribly scarred God's image.

We hate to be told that man is a sinner. Nothing so insults modern man's pride. We have tried desperately to find other words—error of nature, absence of good, false concept of mind —to explain the sin of man. Turning to depth psychology, we attempt to dismiss sin as the result of inner conflicts, inhibitions, or a battle between the "id" and the "super-ego." These concepts only serve to remind us that engulfing human nature is a tragic, threefold estrangement by which man is separated from himself, his neighbors, and his God. There is a corruption in man's will.

. . . Grace. Man is a sinner in need of God's forgiving grace. This is not deadening pessimism; it is Christian realism.

SIT-INS

In sitting down at the lunch counters, they (protesting Negro students) are in reality standing up for the best in the American dream.

In a real sense the "sit-ins" represent more than a demand for service; they represent a demand for respect.

SLAVERY

The immorality of slavery degraded the white master as well as the Negro.

The whole system of slavery was largely perpetuated by sincere though spiritually ignorant persons.

One hundred and fifty years ago, when the Negro was a thing, a chattel whose body belonged to his white master, there were certain slaveowners who worked out arrangements whereby a slave could purchase himself, and become a "freedman." . . . "Help me buy my mother," or "Help me buy my child," was a poignant appeal. It brought the deep torture of black people's souls into stark and shocking focus for many whites to whom the horror of slavery had been emotionally remote.

Many poor whites . . . were the derivative victims of slavery. As long as labor was cheapened by the involuntary servitude of the black man, the freedom of white labor, especially in the South, was little more than a myth. It was free only to bargain from the depressed base imposed by slavery upon the whole labor market.

Throughout slavery, the Negro was treated in a very inhuman fashion. He was considered a thing to be used, not a person to be respected. He was merely a depersonalized cog in a vast plantation machine.

The tragedy of physical slavery was that it gradually led to the paralysis of mental slavery.

SLUMS

Slums are smoldering and seething. It would have been wiser for white America to have seen for itself that slums were intolerable and disbursed them. But many white people of even reasonably good will simply know too little of the agony of ghetto existence to make slums as dispensable as segregated lunch counters. People of ill will still stubbornly cling to the determination to maintain a double standard of social and economic justice.

Slums with hundreds of thousands of living units are not eradicated as easily as lunch counters or buses are integrated.

SOCIAL CHANGE

Negroes *need* an international *detente,* because in a period of tensions and crisis their needs are easily forgotten, and a political rigidity grips the nation that sharply inhibits social change.

The nonviolent approach provides an answer to the long debated question of gradualism versus immediacy. On the one hand it prevents one from falling into the sort of patience which is an excuse for do-nothingism and escapism, ending up in standstillism. On the other hand it saves one from the irresponsible words which estrange without reconciling and the hasty judgment which is blind to the necessities of social progress. It recognizes the need for moving toward the goal of justice with wise restraint and calm reasonableness. But it also recognizes the immorality of slowing up in the move toward justice and capitulating to the guardians of an unjust status quo. It recognizes that social change cannot come overnight. But it causes one to work as if it were a possibility the next morning.

. . . **South.** We have come to believe that the combining of concrete demands, flexibly handled, with mass community involvement, all conducted with nonviolent direct action, is the formula for accomplishment in the South.

SOCIAL CONFLICT

Social conflict is not the product of skilled agitation.

SOCIAL JUSTICE

I have the audacity to believe that peoples everywhere can have three meals a day for their bodies, education and culture for their minds, and dignity, equality and freedom for their spirits. I believe that what self-centered men have torn down men other-centered can build up.

SOCIAL MOVEMENTS

There is no tactical theory so neat that a revolutionary struggle for a share of power can be won merely by pressing a row of buttons. Human beings with all their faults and strengths constitute the mechanism of a social movement. They must make mistakes and learn from them, make more mistakes and learn anew. They must taste defeat as well as success, and discover how to live with each. Time and action are the teachers.

The biggest job in getting any movement off the ground is to keep together the people who form it. This task requires more than a common aim: it demands a philosophy that wins and holds the people's allegiance; and it depends upon open channels of communication between the people and their leaders.

SOCIAL TRANSITION

The present crisis in race relations has characteristics that come to the forefront in any period of social transition. The guardians of the status quo lash out with denunciation against the person or organization that they consider most responsible for the emergence of the new order. Often this denunciation rises to major proportions. In the transition from slavery to restricted emancipation Abraham Lincoln was assassinated. In the present transition from segregation to desegregation the Supreme Court is castigated and the NAACP is maligned and subjected to extralegal reprisals.

SOUTH

The . . . (South) had marvelous possibilities, and once it came to itself and removed the blight of racial segregation, it would experience a moral, political, and economic boom hardly paralleled by any other section of the country.

Who can best lead the South out of the social and economic quagmire? Her native sons. Those who were born and bred on her rich and fertile soil; those who love her because they were nurtured by her. Through love, patience, and understanding good will they can call their brothers to a way of noble living. This hour represents a great opportunity for the white moderates, if they will only speak the truth, obey the law, and suffer if necessary for what they know is right.

Too many politicians in the South . . . make inflammatory statements and disseminate distortions and half-truths which arouse abnormal fears and morbid antipathies within the minds of uneducated and underprivileged whites, leaving them so confused that they are led to acts of meanness and violence which no normal person commits.

. . . Changing. It is deeply significant that a powerful financial and industrial force has emerged in some southern regions, which is prepared to tolerate change in order to avoid costly chaos. This group in turn permits the surfacing of middle-class elements who are further splitting the monolithic front of segregation. Southern church, labor and human-relations groups today articulate sentiments that only yesterday would have been pronounced treasonable in the region. Nevertheless, a deeply entrenched social force, convinced that it need yield nothing of substantial importance, continues to dominate southern life.

. . . **Courts.** No one can understand the feeling that comes to a Southern Negro on entering a federal court unless he sees with his own eyes and feels with his own soul the tragic sabotage of justice in the city and state courts of the South. The Negro goes into these courts knowing that the cards are stacked against him. Here he is virtually certain to face a prejudiced jury or a biased judge, and is openly robbed with little hope of redress. But the Southern Negro goes into the federal court with the feeling that he has an honest chance of justice before the law.

. . . **Desegregation.** At the current rate it will take 93 more years to desegregate the public schools of the South.

. . . **Extremists.** Unfortunately today, the leadership of the white South is by and large in the hands of close-minded extremists. These persons gain prominence and power by the dissemination of false ideas, and by appealing to the deepest fears and hates within the human mind. But they do not speak for the South; of that I am convinced. They speak only for a willful and vocal minority.

. . . **Industrial.** The new South, with its local needs and with an eye to its national image, could not adhere to the brutal, terroristic overseer psychology of bygone days. For these reasons Atlanta, Savannah and some cities of Florida are markedly different from the underdeveloped belts of Mississippi, Louisiana and Albama.

. . . **Law Enforcement.** We find ourselves in a society where the supreme law of the land, the Constitution, is rendered inoperative in vast areas of the nation. State, municipal and county laws and practices negate constitutional mandates as blatantly as if each community were an independent medieval duchy.

In the South we have had a double blow. We have had the mob against us as well as in some instances law enforcement agents actually and literally supporting the mob.

. . . **Lawlessness.** People often wonder why Southern demonstrations tend to sputter out after a vigorous beginning and heroic sacrifice. The answer, simply and inescapably, is that naked force has defeated the Negro. A ruling state apparatus, accustomed for generations to act with impunity against him, is able to employ every element of unchecked power. A slow-moving federal suit, or sporadic and frequently ineffectual federal mediation, is scarcely more adequate to support the Negro in such a one-sided engagement than would be a pat on the back.

Legislation, commissions, bi-racial committees, cannot change a community when those in the seats of power locally are aware that they can organize and employ force while the federal power temporizes.

Federal law is so extensively defied in the South that it is no exaggeration to say that the federal union is barely a reality. For the Southern Negro it is more a tragic myth. He has been exploited, jailed and even murdered, by deeds which federal writ can reach, but his oppression continues essentially unrelieved.

. . . **Negro Voting Rights.** The voting rights bill came into being to end not only discrimination in its overt expressions of voter registration, but also to remove the atmosphere for intimidation, for economic reprisals and for the creation of fear that cause people not to vote. One of the things we have found is that when you have federal registrars in communities, many more Negroes go out to register because they see a different atmosphere and are not over-arched or under-girded with the fear of intimidation and economic reprisals as much as they have in dealing with some of the local registrars that they have dealt with so long.

So far, 3,400 Negroes have been arrested in Selma (Alabama), placing ten times as many in Selma jails as are on the voters' roll.

The heart of the voting problem lies in the fact that the machinery for enforcing this basic right is in the hands of state-appointed officials answerable to the very people who believe they can continue to wield power in the South so long as the Negro is disenfranchised.

Southern officials, knowing they cannot jail citizens for seeking the right to vote, instead claim that Negroes are guilty of other "offenses." In Selma, for instance, more than 3,000 arrests have been made on such charges as "breach of peace," "contempt of court," "disorderly conduct," "unlawful assembly," "contributing to the delinquency of minors," and "criminal provocation."

. . . **Police Brutality.** Police brutality, with community support, or at best indifference, is a daily experience for Negroes in all too many areas of the South. They live in a police state which, paradoxically, maintains itself within a democratic republic.

. . . **School Integration.** Massive, scornful and notorious resistance to law has taken place. The contempt is naked. The sad statistics are so clear: In the South as a whole there is integration of only 443 out of 2,256 school districts with students of both races, and not more than two per cent of all Negroes in southern schools attend classes with white students.

. . . **Segregation.** The legislative halls of the South still ring loud with such words as "interposition" and "nullification." Many public officials are using the power of their offices to defy the law of the land. Through their irresponsible actions, their inflammatory statements, and their dissemination of distortions and half-truths, they have succeeded in arousing abnormal fears and morbid antipathies within the minds of underprivileged and uneducated whites, leaving them in such a state of excitement and confusion that they are led to acts of meanness and violence that no normal person would commit.

(The South) is retarded by a blight that debilitates not only the Negro but also the white man. Poor white men, women, and children, bearing the scars of ignorance, deprivation, and poverty, are evidence of the fact that harm to one is injury to all. Segregation has placed the whole South socially, educationally, and economically behind the rest of the nation.

. . . **Transition.** The present tension in the South is a necessary phase of the transition from an obnoxious negative peace, in which the Negro passively accepted his unjust plight, to a substantive and positive peace, in which all men will respect the dignity and worth of human personality.

. . . **Voter Registration.** Selma (Alabama) has succeeded in limiting Negro registration to the snail's pace of about 145 persons a year. At this rate it would take about 103 years to register the 15,000 eligible Negro voters of Dallas County, not counting those who will reach voting age in that period or who may move into the County.

SOUTHERN RESISTANCE

I feel that we are now moving toward the last days of the strong resistance in the South. I can't say exactly how many years, but I do feel that the forces of resistance are on their last legs and that, in a few years, even in the most recalcitrant state, the officials will recognize that it is necessary to come to terms with what is now the law of the land, and what is necessary to become a reality if we are to survive.

SUFFERING

We must somehow believe that unearned suffering is redemptive.

American Negroes must come to the point where they can say to their white brothers, paraphrasing the words of Gandhi: "We endure suffering. We will meet your physical force with soul force."

It is becoming clear that the Negro is in for a season of suffering. As victories for civil rights mount in the federal courts, angry passions and deep prejudices are further aroused.

. . . I pray that, recognizing the necessity of suffering, the Negro will make of it a virtue. To suffer in a righteous cause is to grow to our humanity's full stature.

Suffering can be a most creative and powerful social force. . . . Both violence and nonviolence agree that suffering can be a very powerful social force. But there is this difference: violence says that suffering can be a powerful social force by inflicting the suffering on somebody else; so this is what we do in war, this is what we do in the whole violent thrust of the violent movement. It believes that you achieve some end by inflicting suffering on another. The nonviolent say that suffering becomes a powerful social force when you willingly accept that violence on yourself, so that selfsuffering stands at the center of the nonviolent movement and the individuals involved are able to suffer in a creative manner, feeling that unearned suffering is redemptive, and that suffering may serve to transform the social situation.

SUPERSTITION

The belief that God will do everything for man is as untenable as the belief that man can do everything for himself. . . . We must learn that to expect God to do everything while we do nothing is not faith, but superstition.

SYSTEMS

. . . and Individuals. One seeks to defeat the unjust system, rather than individuals who are caught in that system. And one goes on believing that somehow this is the important thing, to get rid of the evil system and not the individual who happens to be misguided, who happens to be misled, who was taught wrong. The thing to do is to get rid of the system and thereby create a moral balance within society.

TENSION

The present tensions represent the necessary pains that accompany the birth of anything new. . . . It is both historically and biologically true that there can be no birth and growth without birth pains and growing pains. Whenever there is the emergence of the new, we confront the recalcitrance of the old. So the tensions which we witness in the world today are indicative of the fact that a new world order is being born and an old order is passing away.

When our days become dreary with low-hovering clouds and our nights become darker than a thousand midnights, we will know that we are living in the creative turmoil of a genuine civilization struggling to be born.

I am not afraid of the word "tension." I have earnestly opposed violent tension, but there is a type of constructive, nonviolent tension which is necessary for growth. Just as Socrates felt that it was necessary to create a tension in the mind so that individuals could rise from the bondage of myths and half-truths to the unfettered realm of creative analysis and objective appraisal, so must we see the need for nonviolent gadflies to create the kind of tension in society that will help men rise from the dark depths of prejudice and racism to the majestic heights of understanding and brotherhood.

THOUGHT

Rarely do we find men who willingly engage in hard, solid thinking. There is an almost universal quest for easy answers and half-baked solutions. Nothing pains some people more than having to think.

TOGETHERNESS

The New World is a world of geographical togetherness. This means that no individual or nation can live alone. We must all learn to live together, or we will be forced to die together.

TOKENISM

Many firms (in 1963) found themselves under fire, not because they employed Negroes, but because they did not. Accustomed to ignoring the question, they were forced by its sudden overwhelming presence into a hasty search for absolving tokens. A well-trained Negro found himself sought out by industry for the first time.

Tokenism is a promise to pay. Democracy, in its finest sense, is payment.

While Negroes were being appointed to some significant jobs, and social hospitality was being extended at the White House to Negro leaders, the dreams of the masses remained in tatters. The Negro felt that he recognized the same old bone that had been tossed to him in the past—only now it was being handed to him on a platter, with courtesy.

The Negro has . . . become aware that token integration was not a start in good faith but a new form of discrimination covered up with certain niceties.

Many areas of the South are retreating to a position where they will permit a handful of Negroes to attend all-white schools or allow the employment in lily-white factories of one Negro to a thousand whites. Thus, we have advanced in some places from all-out, unrestrained resistance to a sophisticated form of delaying tactics, embodied in tokenism.

The key question now confronting the nation is whether a swiftly transforming society is to be permitted to give tokens to the Negro while the white population ascends to new levels of social development.

. . . **School Desegregation.** When the Supreme Court modified its decision on school desegregation by approving the Pupil Placement Law, it permitted tokenism to corrupt its intent. It meant that Negroes could be handed the glitter of metal symbolizing the true coin, and authorizing a short-term trip toward democracy. But he who sells you the token instead of the coin always retains the power to revoke its worth, and to command you to get off the bus before you have reached your destination.

TRUTH

The forces of evil may temporarily conquer truth, but truth will ultimately conquer its conqueror.

I still believe that standing up for the truth of God is the greatest thing in the world. This is the end of life.

TYRANNY

Because sin exists on every level of man's existence, the death of one tyranny is followed by the emergence of another tyranny.

··U··

UNEMPLOYMENT

Jobs are harder to create than voting rolls.

. . . **Danger.** There is nothing more dangerous than to develop a large segment of people in (a) society who feel that they have no stake in it, who feel that they have nothing to lose. And so I think joblessness is one of the most serious problems facing the North.

. . . **Negro.** Years back, the Negro could boast that 350,000 of his race were employed by the railroads. Today, less than 50,000 work in this area of transportation. This is but a symbol of what has happened in the coal mines, the steel mills, the packing houses, in all industries that once employed large numbers of Negroes. The livelihood of millions had dwindled down to a frightening fraction because the unskilled and the semiskilled jobs they filled have disappeared under the magic of automation. In that separate culture of poverty in which the half-educated Negro lives, an economic depression rages today. To deal with this disaster by opening some doors to all, and all doors to some, amounts merely to organizing chaos.

UNIFORMITY

Unity has never meant uniformity. If it had, it would not have been possible for such dedicated democrats, as Thomas Jefferson and George Washington, a radical such as Thomas Paine and an autocrat such as Alexander Hamilton to lead a unified American Revolution.

UNITY

There is amazing power in unity. Where there is true unity, every effort to disunite only serves to strengthen the unity.

UNIVERSE

This universe is not a tragic expression of meaningless chaos but a marvelous display of orderly cosmos.

. . . **Purpose.** Materialistic philosophy leads inevitably into a dead-end street in an intellectually senseless world. To believe that human personality is the result of the fortuitous interplay of atoms and electrons is as absurd as to believe that a monkey by hitting typewriter keys at random will eventually produce a Shakespearean play.

Irreligion . . . would have us believe that we are orphans cast into the terrifying immensities of space in a universe that is without purpose or intelligence. Such a view drains courage and exhausts the energies of men.

VALUES

We are prone to judge success by the index of our salaries or the size of our automobiles, rather than by the quality of our service and relationship to humanity.

We must make a choice. Will we continue to march to the drumbeat of conformity and respectability, or will we, listening to the beat of a more distant drum, move to its echoing sounds? Will we march only to the music of time, or will we, risking criticism and abuse, march to the soul-saving music of eternity?

Living in the colony of time, we are ultimately responsible to the empire of eternity. As Christians we must never surrender our supreme loyalty to any time-bound custom or earth-bound idea.

Moral principles have lost their distinctiveness. For modern man, absolute right and absolute wrong is a matter of what the majority is doing. Right and wrong are relative to likes and dislikes and the customs of a particular community. We have unconsciously applied Einstein's theory of relativity, which properly described the physical universe, to the moral and ethical realm.

The means by which we live have outdistanced the ends for which we live. Our scientific power has outrun our spiritual power. We have guided missiles and misguided men. Like the rich man of old, we have foolishly minimized the internal of our lives and maximized the external. We have absorbed life in livelihood.

There is so much frustration in the world because we have relied on gods rather than God. We have genuflected before the god of science only to find that it has given us the atomic bomb, producing fears and anxieties that science can never mitigate. We have worshipped the god of pleasure only to discover that thrills play out and sensations are short-lived. We have bowed before the god of money only to learn that there are such things as love and friendship that money cannot buy and that in a world of possible depressions, stock market crashes, and bad business investments, money is a rather uncertain deity. These transitory gods are not able to save or bring happiness to the human heart. Only God is able. It is faith in him that we must rediscover.

VICTORY

At Bunker Hill the British won the hill, but the colonists won their self-respect and the profound respect of their enemy. . . . The vanquished won the war on that hill—the victors lost it. Birmingham was different only in the sense that the Negroes did not retreat, and they won some significant gains. The desegregation of lunch counters, libraries, schools on a token basis may seem a small breach in the enormous fortress of injustice, but considering the strength of the fortress, it was a towering achievement. And Birmingham did more than this. It was a fuse—it detonated a revolution that went on to win scores of other victories.

VIETNAM

Negroes and poor people generally are bearing the heaviest burden of this (Vietnam) war.

If America's soul becomes totally poisoned, part of the autopsy must read Vietnam.

VIOLENCE

A philosophy of nonviolent resistance . . . is simply a refusal, in a nonviolent sense, to cooperate with the evil of segregation. We, as a race, cannot think in terms of retaliatory violence. The attempt to use the method of violence in our struggle would be both impractical and immoral. Violence creates many more problems than it solves. There is a voice through the vista of time saying: "He who lives by the sword shall perish by the sword." History is replete with the bleached bones of nations which failed to follow this truth. So we decided to choose nonviolence.

I think a turn to violence on the part of the Negro . . . would be both impractical and immoral.

Predictions (of violence) are always a conscious or unconscious invitation to action.

Violence ends by defeating itself. It creates bitterness in the survivors and brutality in the destroyers.

When people, especially in public office, talk about bloodshed as a concomitant of integration, they stir and arouse the hoodlums to acts of destruction, and often work under cover to bring them about.

Violence often brings about momentary results. Nations have frequently won their independence in battle. But in spite of temporary victories, violence never brings permanent peace. It solves no social problem; it merely creates new and more complicated ones.

Violence is immoral because it thrives on hatred rather than love. It destroys community and makes brotherhood impossible. It leaves society in monologue rather than dialogue.

If the American Negro and other victims of oppression succumb to the temptation of using violence in the struggle for freedom, future generations will be the recipients of a desolate night of bitterness, and our chief legacy to them will be an endless reign of meaningless chaos. Violence is not the way.

The Negro in the South in 1955, assessing the power of the forces arrayed against him, could not perceive the slightest prospect of victory in (the violent) approach. He was unarmed, unorganized, untrained, disunited and, most important, psychologically and morally unprepared for the deliberate spilling of blood. Although his desperation had prepared him with the courage to die for freedom if necessary, he was not willing to commit himself to racial suicide with no prospect of victory.

The Negro turned his back on force not only because he knew he could not win his freedom through physical force but also because he believed that through physical force he could lose his soul.

Violence as a way of achieving racial justice is both impractical and immoral. It is impractical because it is a descending spiral ending in destruction for all. . . . It is immoral because it seeks to humiliate the opponent rather than his understanding; it seeks to annihiliate rather than convert.

Civilization and violence are antithetical concepts.

When there is justice and the pursuit of justice, violence appears, and where there is injustice and frustration, the potentialities for violence are greater, and I would like to strongly stress the point that the more we can achieve victories through nonviolence, the more it will be possible to keep the nonviolent discipline at the center of the movement. But the more we find individuals facing conditions of frustration, conditions of disappointment and seething despair as a result of the slow pace of things and the failure to change conditions, the more it will be possible for the apostles of violence to interfere.

The minute the nomenclature of violence gets into the atmosphere, people begin to respond violently, and in their unsophisticated minds they cannot quite make the distinction between defensive and aggressive violence.

. . . **Defensive and Aggressive.** On the question of defensive violence, . . . I don't think we need programmatic action around defensive violence. People are going to defend themselves anyway. I think the minute you have programmatic action around defensive violence and pronouncements about it, the line of demarcation between defensive violence and aggressive violence becomes very thin.

. . . **Law Enforcement.** We know that violence develops in the whole racial struggle only when the violent forces feel they have support and that they are aided and abetted by the law-enforcement agencies. Wherever the law-enforcement agencies and the public officials have made it clear that they would not have violence, it hasn't emerged.

VOTING

Americans of good will have learned that no nation can long continue to flourish or to find its way to a better society while it allows any one of its citizens, let alone vast numbers in eleven southern states, to be denied the right to participate in the most fundamental of all privileges of democracy—the right to vote.

At a time when the Supreme Court has said that the law of the land demands "one man, one vote," so that all state legislatures may be democratically structured, it would be a mockery indeed if this were not followed without delay by an insistence upon "one vote for every man."

. . . **Literacy Tests.** It is surely ironical that the states which have labored so diligently to keep the Negro masses ignorant through inferior segregated education now require "literacy" as a prerequisite for voting. You hardly need much formal training to know who as sheriff will treat you like a human being and who will crack your skull!

. . . **Negro.** Today, a shift in the Negro vote could upset the outcome of several state contests, and affect the result of a Presidential election.

Voting is more than a badge of citizenship and dignity—it is an effective tool for change. Voting is the foundation stone for political action. With it the Negro can eventually vote out of office public officials who bar the doorway to decent housing, public safety, jobs and decent integrated education. It is now obvious that the basic elements so vital to Negro advancement can only be achieved by seeking redress from government at local, state and federal levels. To do this the vote is essential.

Voting as a badge of full citizenship has always had a special meaning for the Negro.

. . . **Power.** Southern seniority in Congress, resting as it does on the "whites only" ballot box, maintains power in the hands of our nation's most reactionary politicians. Bills providing for the welfare of our nation, from medicare to education, must run the gantlet of southern power before they are en-acted—and many never are.

. . . **South.** Alabama law gives the (voting) registrars wide discretionary powers. At the registration office are separate lines and separate tables for voters according to race. The registrars servicing Negro lines move at a noticeably leisurely pace, so that of fifty Negroes in line, as few as fifteen may be reached by the end of the day. All voters are required to fill out a long questionnaire as a test of eligibility. Often Negroes fill out the questionnaire at several different times before they have been informed that they have done so successfully.

WAGE

. . . **Minimum.** It is easy to conceive of a plan to raise the minimum wage and thus in a single stroke extract millions of people from poverty. But between the conception and the realization there lies a formidable wall.

WAR

Casualties of war keep alive postwar bitterness.

While war could never be a positive or absolute good, it could serve as a negative good in the sense of preventing the spread and growth of an evil force. War, horrible as it is, might be preferable to surrender to a totalitarian system—Nazi, Fascist, or Communist.

When Jesus says "Love your enemies," he is setting forth a profound and ultimately inescapable admonition. Have we not come to such an impasse in the modern world that we must love our enemies—or else? The chain reaction of evil—hate begetting hate, wars producing more wars—must be broken, or we shall be plunged into the dark abyss of annihilation.

If we assume that mankind has a right to survive, then we must find an alternative to war and destruction. In our day of space vehicles and guided ballistic missiles, the choice is either nonviolence or nonexistence.

There is an element of urgency in our redirecting of American power. We still have a choice: nonviolent coexistence or violent co-annihilation. It is still not too late to make the proper choice.

A so-called limited war will leave little more than a calamitous legacy of human suffering, political turmoil, and spiritual disillusionment. A world war—God forbid!—will leave only smouldering ashes as a mute testimony of a human race whose folly led inexorably to untimely death.

. . . **Armaments.** The potential destructiveness of modern weapons totally rules out the possibility of war ever again achieving a negative good.

. . . **Fear.** We say that war is a consequence of hate, but close scrutiny reveals this sequence: first fear, then hate, then war, and finally deeper hatred. Were a nightmarish nuclear war to engulf our world, the cause would be not so much that one nation hated another, but that both nations feared each other.

. . . **Vietnam.** The promises of the Great Society have been shot down on the battlefield of Vietnam.

The pursuit of this widened war (Vietnam) has narrowed domestic welfare programs, making the poor, white and Negro, bear the heaviest burdens both at the front and at home. . . . The . . . war budget alone is more than five times the amount committed to antipoverty programs.

WASHINGTON MARCH

The enormous multitude (at the civil rights march on Washington) was the living, beating heart of an infinitely noble movement. It was an army without guns, but not without strength. It was an army into which no one had to be drafted. It was white and Negro, and of all ages. It had adherents of every faith, members of every class, every profession, every political party, united by a single ideal. It was a fighting army, but no one could mistake that its most powerful weapon was love.

In its entire glittering history, Washington had never seen a spectacle of the size and grandeur that assembled there on August 28, 1963. (The civil rights march on Washington.) Among the nearly 250,000 people who journeyed that day to the capital, there were many dignitaries and many celebrities, but the stirring emotion came from the mass of ordinary people who stood in majestic dignity as witnesses to their single-minded determination to achieve democracy in their time.

WEALTH

Wealth always comes as a result of the commonwealth.

Jesus never made a sweeping indictment against wealth. Rather, he condemned the misuse of wealth.

. . . **Distribution.** God intends that all of his children shall have the basic necessities for meaningful, healthful life. Surely it is unchristian and unethical for some to wallow in the soft beds of luxury while others sink in the quicksands of poverty.

WEALTH AND POVERTY

Nothing in wealth is inherently vicious, and nothing in poverty is inherently virtuous.

WHITE BACKLASH

White backlash . . . for the most part . . . was powered by petulance rather than principle. Therefore, when the American people saw before them a clear choice between a future of progress with racial justice or stagnation with ancient privilege, they voted in landslide proportions for justice.

WHITE CITIZENS COUNCIL

The White Citizens Council's . . . actions . . . extended far beyond the bounds of the law. Their methods were the methods of open and covert terror, brutal intimidation, and threats of starvation to Negro men, women, and children. They took open economic reprisals against whites who dared to protest their defiance of the law, and the aim of their boycotts was not merely to impress their victims but to destroy them if possible.

WHITE SUPREMACY

With the growth of urban society the folkways of white supremacy will gradually pass away.

Many of the problems today are due to a futile attempt by the white South to maintain a system of human values that came into being under a feudalistic plantation system and that cannot survive in a democratic age.

The causal basis for the system of slavery must to a large extent be traced back to the economic factor. Men convinced themselves that a system which was so economically profitable must be morally justifiable. They formulated elaborate theories of racial superiority. Their rationalizations clothed obvious wrongs in the beautiful garments of righteousness. This tragic attempt to give moral sanction to an economically profitable system gave birth to the doctrine of white supremacy.

WORLD UNITY

We cannot long survive spiritually separated in a world that is geographically together.

Men of all races and nations are today challenged to be neighborly. The call for a worldwide good-neighbor policy is more than an ephemeral shibboleth; it is the call to a way of life which will transform our imminent cosmic elegy into a psalm of creative fulfillment.

WORSHIP

Worship at its best is a social experience in which people from all levels of life come together to affirm their oneness and unity under God.